Signposts
to
Manifestation

Publications
+234-813-529-1769, +234-809-481-4575

Kunle Akinbowale

Signposts *to* Manifestation

How To Live A Consistently Overcoming Life

Kunle Akinbowale

Kunle Akinbowale

ISBN: 978-1984287038

First Edition, 2017

Unless otherwise indicated, all scripture quotations
are from the New King James Version of the Holy Bible.

Contact The Author
Kunle Akinbowale
Kunleakinbowalebooks@gmail.com

Published In Nigeria By
SOS Publications
+234-813-529-1769, +234-809-481-4575
sospublications@yahoo.com

DEDICATION

This book is dedicated my Creator for His countless blessings evident in my life.

Kunle Akinbowale

ACKNOWLEDGMENT

Sincere appreciation goes to all members of my family and glorious people of the Love of Christ Chapel International Ministries.

Kunle Akinbowale

TABLE OF CONTENT

Kunle Akinbowale

PREFACE

I have seen servants on horses, while princes walk on the ground like servants. Ecclesiastes 10:7

Our introductory Scripture is a disappointing one. We live in a time and age where the Scripture above is literally being fulfilled. We see thousands of believers living far below God.s miraculous provisions and divine expectation for them. There are bountifully great privileges available in Christ, yet too many Christians are struggling to live above the status quo. This is a disappointing disorder.

The Scripture says we are God.s workmanship, created in Christ Jesus for good works, which God prepared beforehand that we should walk in them (Ephesians 2:10). God prepared good works for us beforehand; before we were ever born.

But because we were lost in sin we could not do those good works outside of Jesus Christ. Then God redeemed us through Christ Jesus so that we can walk in those good works.

If you are in Christ Jesus, you are not expected to sit around looking for good works to walk in. You already have good work prepared for you to walk in. Good works are works that show forth God.s glory and honour you, His child. Good work was Jesus Christ opening the eyes of the blind, raising the dead, cleansing the leper, and bringing salvation to sinners. The more He did this, the more the kingdom of darkness was bashed and the more God was glorified. No wonder towards the end of His earthly life Jesus said, I have finished the work which you (God) have given me to do (John 17:4).

Have you even started the work God has given you to do? Have you started to live the life in Christ Jesus that victorious life which God wants you to live? Have you started manifesting? Has your light started to shine so significantly that men are seeing your good works and are glorifying your Father in heaven? Are you turning your office upside down with righteous living such that wicked men who embezzle company.s money are saying, "Hey, he has come again. He will expose our secrets to the management."

You can never live the life God has called you to live and you will not manifest. It is not possible. What follows a genuine life in Christ Jesus is manifestation. Men will see your good works and will glorify your Father in heaven. After Jesus had been tested in the wilderness, the Bible says He came out full of the Spirit and power and His fame grew far and wide thereafter (Luke 4:14). Jesus began to manifest as soon as He had entered into the life He came here on earth to live.

The Bible says we are complete in Christ Jesus Who is the Head of principalities and powers (Col. 2:10). The Living Bible translation of that same Scripture says we have all things in Christ Jesus. If truly we have all things in Christ Jesus, why then do we find too many believers living terribly below the life that God has ordained for them to live; both spiritually and financially?

I once read the story of a poor beggar who was found dead in his ramshackle apartment. He was known to be a popular beggar around the area, but when his dead body was found and his body searched, a purse with thousands of dollars was tied around his waist. This beggar had all the money he needed to live a comfortable life, yet he died poor.

Are you living below the life that God has ordained for you? Are you actualizing the victories God wants you to have, since God, in Christ Jesus, has attained all these victories for you? Are you becoming everything you are supposed to become in Christ Jesus so that God.s name may be glorified through your manifestation?

If God has designed that you should manifest and you are not manifesting, you are living below God.s purposeful design for your life. This may be due to your ignorance of these great blessings or due to the works of your enemy, the devil.

A life that manifests is a life that shines the way God expects His children to shine. The Scripture says let your light so shine before men that they may see your good works and glorify your Father in heaven (Matthew 5:16). When your life as a Christian begins to become a wonder to unbelievers, then you are manifesting. When everything you touch at your place of work literally succeeds, you are manifesting (Genesis 39:2-3). When men cannot get anything done unless you are around and available, you are manifesting (1 Samuel 16:11). When what you say becomes "law", even though you are just a subordinate at that place where you are, you are manifesting (Genesis 41:37-39).

If you have been living below this God-designed expectation for your life, God is saying it is time for you to move up and move on, because you have dwelt too long around this mountain. It is time for you to begin to actualize every single promise and privilege He has provided for you through your salvation in Christ Jesus. It is time for you to stop living lesser than He created you and start to conform to the miraculous life He has designed you to live; whether spiritually, emotionally, mentally, physically, or financially.

This is because the life of the Christian is the life of the miraculous. Anywhere he is, he is a miracle. Just as Paul.s presence on that ship saved the people on the ship and Joseph.s presence in Egypt saved the whole world from famine, your presence wherever you are, as a child of God, should create a revolutionary turnaround right there.

It is my prayer that the Holy Spirit will, by the pages of this book, create a fiery reaction within you that will cause you to see where you are with anger and charge you to begin to gravitate towards where you are supposed to be; so that you can become everything God has predestined you to be in Him.

It is your season to manifest.

Pastor Kunle Akinbowale

Chapter One

THE JOURNEY INTO MANIFESTATION

For the earnest expectation of the creation eagerly waits for the revealing of the sons of God. Romans 8:19

What is manifestation? Manifestation is a public expression of what was formerly hidden. Manifestation is to show off, to be in an enviable position, to have something that can be expressed publicly. If a thing can manifest, it means the thing has an intrinsic potential to manifest, though it may not be manifesting.

17

I would like to start this chapter by saying that you have the potential to manifest. Although you may not be manifesting at the moment, although you may not even look anywhere close to anyone who can ever manifest, although the situations around you are so contrary to what I am writing about here, you have the capacity to manifest; and this capacity is made available for you because you belong to Christ Jesus.

It is your right to access God.s grace with ease so that you will become what God has called you to be. You cannot manifest when you are struggling. An unbeliever is permitted to struggle financially but you are not permitted to. It only took a word from God and Isaac.s situation changed within a year (Genesis 26:12-13). But you will never read a single place where it was mentioned that Isaac toiled that year. No. God simply spoke to Isaac and Isaac did what God said, and that same year, Isaac reaped more than he could ever imagine. So, potentially, you have in you what it takes to manifest, but only waiting for that one word or direction from God, and your manifestation will be activated. You are definitely more than the life you are currently exhibiting. Your potentials are yet to me actualized.

Unbelievers are guaranteed to struggle. In fact, unbelievers must always struggle to make ends meet because they do not have God for their help. But your Father says in Isaiah 48:17, I am the LORD your God, Who teaches you to profit, Who leads you by the way you should go. He is the LORD your God Who holds your hand and makes you succeed. That is why Isaac could succeed in one year, until the owners of the land even became envious of him (Genesis 26:14).

Let.s read Roman 8:19,

> **For the earnest expectation of the creation eagerly waits for the revealing of the sons of God.**

Can you notice that there is a waiting in the Scripture above? Who is waiting? The world is waiting. They are waiting for the manifestation of the sons of God. But how long do you want them to wait?

Let.s read the scripture from the Amplified translation:

> **For [even the whole] creation (all nature) waits expectantly and longs earnestly for God.s sons to be made known [waits for the revealing, the disclosing of their sonship].**

They are waiting for the disclosure of the sons of God. They really want the sons of God to manifest. They are in dire need of solution which can only be made available by the Sons of God and indeed the world cannot wait any longer, so they are interested in the quick and real manifestation of the Sons of God. The earth groans and moans under the weight of wickedness and is constantly looking for the sons of light to bring righteousness to bear on the land. But as long as the sons of righteousness will not take their rightful place, this evil will continue.

People of the world have expectations. They

are constantly waiting, and that waiting will continue as long as you, a child of God, will not manifest. If in your family things are not properly set right, it is because you are not manifesting. The Bible has said it that everywhere the sole of your feet shall tread, there the Lord has given to you (Joshua 1:3). If you are not taking your workplace for God, you are at fault; not God. If your finances are not growing as they should, you shouldn.t blame God, you should ask yourself what privilege you may not be activating. If they keep passing you over for promotion at your place of work, be absolutely sure it is God.s will before you start to say, It is God.s will that I should not be promoted.

You can manifest in your spiritual life.
You can manifest in your financial life.
You can manifest in your marital life.
You can manifest in your academic life.
You can manifest in your career life.
You can manifest in every area of your life.

Your life can and should be sincerely controlled and influenced by the victories Christ Jesus has achieved for you.

Scripture says that the earnest expectation of the creation waits eagerly and earnestly for the manifestation of God.s children. The world is waiting and so whatever they are waiting for, it means it is worth waiting for, and it means that when that thing comes, there will be a change, and a great relief.

They are waiting. This means that God.s sons have not been made known, so there is an expectation. The whole world is waiting. What are they waiting for? Why is manifestation delayed? Somebody said that, A 70 year old man who buys a bicycle and writes on it faithful are the works of God, what.s special about that?

He buys a bicycle at 70 and He calls God faithful. How long will he live before he would say goodbye to the world? Even our nation.s President would wish he was younger. You can imagine what he would do with the energy if he were younger. There are some things he would wish to do now, at over 73 years, yet he can.t do them, because the strength is no longer there. No wonder the Bible says, it is good for a young man to bear his burden in his youth (Lam. 3:27).

There is something about timing. It is not enough for you to prosper. It is that you should prosper at the right time. A Yoruba prayer says, Do not let me lose my teeth before I have meat. At the time when all the teeth is lost from the mouth, all that.s left for the person to eat is fish, and it must be severely cooked to soften it, so the toothless man can be able to eat it.

I heard about an old woman who ate only twice a day for 20 years. She doesn.t eat dinner, and her breakfast is usually, constantly a combination of pap and bean-cake. Yet at one time in her life, she ate lavishly. You know, there comes a level in all our lives when things change. I pray God will make you to manifest at the right time in Jesus name.

Some people have cars they can never drive again. The cars are there but they can.t drive them again; only their children can drive them. Why is this so? The cars did not come at the time they should have.

23

The Bible says the world is waiting. Look at the time the Bible was written, so long ago. It says the world is waiting for the children of God to manifest. If the world is waiting, then it means they have not stopped waiting. The Bible did not say the world waited. It did not say the world will wait. Rather, it says the world is waiting. This is an ongoing experience.

As you look around on the world today, you will know there is still a waiting. The world constantly wants more lights to conquer the darkness that is enveloping several spheres of life. You are that light; you are that light that must shine for the world to see, so that darkness can find its place and light can come to stay.

Christ, the Light of the world, has replicated Himself in so many lives so that more lights can shine all over the world. Will you stand up from today to be the light that you are in Christ Jesus?

The disciples were first called Christians in Antioch. Having stayed with the people for

Signposts to Manifestation

one year, the people of Antioch looked at them and they observed that these ones were just like Christ in character (Acts 11:26). They had observed them and one year was enough for them to become fully known to the people of Antioch, and this precipitated their conclusion.

Christianity was not a name that people who call themselves Christians gave themselves. It was a name given to them by their observers. They looked at their manifestation. They looked at them and thought, If we call them little Christ, we cannot be wrong, and thus, they named them. The Bible says these Christians turned the world upside down (Acts 17:6). They shook the world.

It is a popular knowledge in Lagos that if you wanted to have a large occasion that would turn the whole of Lagos upside down, you would not schedule it to take place on the first Friday of every month. Why is this so? This is because the Redeemed Christian Church of God.s monthly Holy Ghost meeting at the Redemption camp holds on that day, and this meeting regularly creates

25

hectic, bumper-to-bumper traffic. Whether the devil likes it or not, this meeting has to be taken into consideration for every occasion anyone in Lagos must have.

I remember overhearing Pastor E.A. Adeboye saying one day, When the first Friday of every month [the day the Holy Ghost meeting holds], is declared a public holiday, only then will I say, God, you can take me. I have finished the work. That is a dream. That is a vision. Someone with such a vision cannot sit down. When people are commending you that you have done much, you will reply, I have not done anything; I am just about to start.

Bishop Benson Idahosa was asked, What is your greatest miracle? He replied, The next one. Every miracle I have done is not the greatest one. The one I will do next is the greatest one. This is the kind of aspiration that will make you never to settle for your present achievement.

Brother Paul said in Philippians 3:19,
Brethren, I do not count myself to have apprehended;

but one thing [I do,] forgetting those things which are behind and reaching forward to those things which are ahead.

There is a need for pressing forward. The whole world expects the manifestation of the sons of God. So, there is a waiting, and it is worth the wait.

Do you know your family is waiting for your manifestation? One of the days, I saw a headline. There was a picture of a woman from an Arab country, and the headline read, Muslim woman gave Jesus one day or two to do something so that she will take a decision. That is what the world is asking. Have you ever heard a worldly person say, If the Lord answers your prayer, then I will follow you.

The world is waiting for the manifestation of the sons of God. Isaiah 60:1-2 says,
Arise, shine; For your light has come! And the glory of the LORD is risen upon you. For behold, the darkness

27

shall cover the earth, And
deep darkness the people;
But the LORD will arise
over you, And His glory will
be seen upon you.

People will be confused and they will say,
There is no way; things are not working for
me, but you will say, Things are working for
me. In Genesis 26:12, the Bible says Isaac
sowed that year and in the same year, he
reaped hundred fold. It was a year when
everybody does not have the same result. It
was a year when people were quitting
businesses. Bankruptcy was becoming the
norm. It was a year when people were
moving from three-bedroom flat to one-
room apartment. It was a year when people
were selling their cars. It was a year when
things were not working for people. That
same year, Isaac sowed in the land and he
reaped hundred folds. Will that not make
the news? Someone said, It takes a new thing
to make the news. The world is waiting for
some news.

You would hear a conversation like this:
Man 1: Did you hear the news

about his house? That he built it in three months?

Man 2: No, I did not.

Man 1: Come with me and I will take you to see the house.

Man 2: Sorry, but that.s not my route.

Man 1: Don.t worry, I will drive you to your destination.

And when they have visited the house,

Man 2: Wow! Did God really do this?

Man 1: God did it for him ooo.

Man 2: Haa! The God Who did this is the God I will follow.

The question is: are you even going to manifest? Are you planning to manifest? The world is waiting. If you are planning to manifest, when are you going to manifest? Why should it not be now? The Bible says, You will arise [and] have mercy on Zion; For the time to favor her, Yes, the set time, has come (Psalms 102:13). It is now. It should not be tomorrow. Why? This is because the faster it comes, the better.

If you become blessed today, you will cover more grounds, than becoming blessed in ten years. time.

Somebody published a picture of our first political leaders who signed Nigeria into existence and I observed that none of those political figures were forty years old at that time when they birthed the country. The two people that founded Guaranty Trust Bank were less than 40 years old. At that age, most people are still searching for jobs.

When you do not think, you settle for some things you should not settle for. Yes, you are carrying the gospel, but the same gospel says you will manifest. It does not also say you will manifest when you become 80 years old. You cannot use a Jeep when you are 80 years old. At that age is the period most old people request for small cars. When you are still young though, you can do own and drive the Jeep.

It is not in doubt that you are destined to be great or that you carry the potential to rule your world. Have you asked yourself, Is this what God really wants for me? I do not know if you have ever asked yourself this. I am sure the answer you will get from God is that I made you to be more than this. The only thing that will stop you from being more than this is your ignorance of Scripture and the wickedness in the world, which God promised He would handle when your way pleases Him. The Bible says: .When a man.s ways please the Lord, He makes his enemies to be at peace with him. (Proverb 16:7)

Jesus prayed, "I do not pray that You should take them out of the world, but that You should keep them from the evil one. (John 17:15). Let the evil be there, but let it not be able to touch them. So, God is not ignorant of the fact that there will be trouble. He knows there will be trouble as long as you are in this world. Jesus said, In the world you will have tribulation; but be of good cheer, I have overcome the world" (John 16:33). They will pursue you but they will not overtake you.

God is aware that there are things that will contend with you. God is going to take care of those things. But the issue is that there are some things God expect us to take care of ourselves and many times, we do not take care of them. This is our problem. And this is why the Scripture says the whole world awaits the manifestation of the sons of God. Please note that the world is not awaiting the manifestation of God, but rather, it awaits the manifestation of the sons of God. So the manifestation being awaited is that from man, not a divine manifestation of sort, that the world can.t relate with as humans.

When a farmer plants a tree and the season for fruits is due, he goes to the tree. Why is this so? Because it is normal for this tree to bring forth fruit. No wonder Jesus told a parable of a man who came to look for fruit on his tree and, finding none, he called his gardener to add more fertilizer, do more work to it, in order that the tree can grow and bear fruit. The man returned the second year and he did more work on the tree. By the third year when he came and found no fruit on the tree, he said, Cut it off. How long shall it continue to just occupy the ground? (Luke 13:7). It is disappointing.

God created you to bring forth fruits.
God is waiting for you to manifest.
The world is waiting for you to manifest.
You will surely manifest, in Jesus name.

There was a time when God told the children of Israel, You have dwelt too long here. It is time to move forward (Deut. 1:6-7). God is not a magician. He will not do for you what you should do for yourself. When the Israelites were going through the Red Sea, God didn.t just let them disappear to the other side. There was a lesson they needed to learn by walking through that Red Sea. God could carry them without them walking, but they needed to walk to learn. They needed to see that the challenge may be there but it could do nothing to them because He (God) was on their side.

The Bible says Work out your own salvation with fear and trembling (Phil. 2:12). Work it out! Work out your breakthrough. Work out your deliverance. Work out your prosperity. Work out your success. There is a working there.

All God did for the people of Israel was to

show them the way to go and to lead them. As they walked through the Red Sea, the water was still a wall of water right on both their sides. Sometimes, God allows us to see the magnitude of the problem so that when He takes care of them, we will understand the greatness of the victory He wrought for us. If the water had cleared off before they got to the Red Sea, they would have downplayed the testimony. Yet, Pharaoh and his army were coming behind them. They could not go forward nor backward. They even told Moses, You just want us to die where there is no burial ground (Exod. 14:11).

They saw the battle coming and the water right in front of them. They could not go sideways either; there were valleys everywhere. They were stuck. At that time, they knew the only way for them was for God to make a way. God told Moses, Tell them to move forward. (Exod. 14:15). Yet, they needed to still walk. Some of them would have thought, No, I won.t go into that water. It could collapse over us when we stepped in. Of course, when they finally walked through, the water collapsed over their enemies. This simply means that God has a way of turning that difficult situation into a pleasant one for you because you need to manifest, but God will not make you to go through a shortcut. There is no shortcut anywhere.

Sometimes, God wants you to go through the challenge full length, but He will be with you. When you pass through the water, He said, I will be with you (Isaiah 43:1-3). He said when. He did not say if. He wants you to know that you will pass through the waters, but you will both pass through it together.

When you are tried, you will come out as gold (Job 23:10). The beauty of this word is when you hold the microphone and sing the praises of God for the good things He has done for you, after He has made you victorious over the Red Sea and the enemy. You can tell people, this is what God has done. You can tell them, I didn.t get here by myself. Grace carried me through.

I worked with a man in 2007 and he was a level ahead of me. He had one role at the time. He left that role and went to another bank, and he got a level ahead. I was a level below him. This man works in one of the first two banks in Nigeria, and he is doing very well financially. Eight years later, as at the time of this writing, he has not moved from that level. I have changed level three times within that same period. The last time we talked, I had to let him know, There is a problem somewhere.

When God asks for results and you do not give Him results, He goes to another person. In the parable of the sower, the same seed planted on different soils produced different results (Mark 4:3-9). The same seed!. Every of the seed had the potential to grow. The difference is the ground. To prove to us that the problem is not with the seed, they all grew. Some grew, but thorns finished them. This further indicates that the seed had the potential to grow, but problems frustrated it. The seed had the potential to grow, but it fell on the wrong soil.

The one that fell on the rock truly wanted to grow but there was no root to carry it. But the one that fell on the good soil brought forth fruits of different kinds. This is what should have become of the other seeds, but for the ground. We are all from one Source, God. Christians are blessed through Abraham (Galatians 3:14). Every Christian has the same Source.

Is God wicked? No. Is God difficult? Never. Will God prefer that one person be rich and another be wretched? No. The same seed is planted in them. What each one does with his seed is what makes a difference. There is no barren land, there are only barren people. When you are barren, you are barren in the head.

Before the scriptures would say they are waiting, it means there is a potential for manifestation in every child of God. Be careful to notice the Bible did not call it the children of God, but the sons of God. there is a difference between children and sons. As many as are led by the Spirit of God are the sons of God (Romans 8:14). So, the sons of God are not churchgoers. The sons of God are people whom God leads.

The starting point is to ask, Am I a son of God? You must first make sure that you are a son of God. When you have become the son of God, then you have the potential to become all you are supposed to be.

The fact that a person did not become what he is made to be does not mean he does not have the potential in him. He only did not activate it. The seed to manifest is in you. God has nothing more to do than what He has done. For you to become anything, God does not have to make any further effort. He has paid a price once and for all, and on the cross of Calvary, He said, It is finished (John 19:30). All that is left is for you to draw upon it. When somebody sends billions of cash into your account, all you have to do is withdraw it; no extra work needed.

Are you going to draw it? The difference between the person who draws it and the person who doesn.t is what you are seeing today. When God is merciful to one, He is merciful to the other. What you do with that mercy is what counts afterwards. It is our heart and what we know about Him that matters.

It is possible to manifest. It is certain that you can manifest. No one can awaken this God-given possibility in you except you. So it is time to muster that inner courage and tell yourself you will stop being less than what God wants you to be and will start to become everything God demands you to be.

Manifestation is an experience God wants for His sons. Are you His son? Then it is your time to manifest.

Chapter Two

WHY MANIFESTATION IS DELAYED

My people are destroyed for lack of knowledge. Because you have rejected knowledge, I also will reject you from being priest for Me; Because you have forgotten the law of your God, I also will forget your children. Hosea 4:6

God called us that we may become something. God called Abraham so that he would become the father of many nations. Even when he was over 90 years, his calling had not changed. Even when he helped God and had another child, God acknowledged that that still wasn.t His plan.

The world is tired of waiting for your manifestation. The more you fail, the more the world looks for substitute; usually, substitutes of the inferior quality. Just imagine how many people you will draw to God if you manifest. Just imagine that you are now the managing director of your company and you declare fellowship meetings on Wednesday. Will the staff object? Of course, no.

Once, I was in a discussion with a friend. He made a very strong point which I would like to note. He said, Kunle, imagine if churches could buy countless numbers of BRT buses for transportation, and they charge just a quarter of what others charge. Say, 20 naira for any destination within Lagos. First of all, if that ever happens, the buses will always be crowded. That would be a good blessing, wouldn.t it? Now, because you have slashed transportation cost drastically that way, if you decide to play Christian messages and songs on those buses, would anyone object to you playing them? Definitely, no. You have an opportunity to win them to Christ.

Now, imagine if the transportation cost is free. The only payment, as it were, is that Christian messages and songs will be played on the bus. Also, imagine that you add powerful private prayers to the audio messages being played on the buses. Wouldn.t the whole of Lagos catch fire that way?

Sadly though, recently, when I was watching African magic on DSTV, a black shade would cover any place where God or Jesus is written in the subtitle. From a simple deduction, they are telling us, As long as it is not a religious program, don.t mention God or Jesus. I thought to myself, This is because Christians are not manifesting. The more the Christian manifests, the more the unbelievers will come to God. When we do not manifest, there will be room for them to go look for other gods.

The sad truth is this: we are not where God wants us to be.

Why is manifestation delayed? We will review the story of two men in this chapter.

1 Kings 19: 15-17 reads:

Then the LORD said to him: "Go, return on your way to the Wilderness of Damascus; and when you arrive, anoint Hazael [as] king over Syria. Also you shall anoint Jehu the son of Nimshi [as] king over Israel. And Elisha the son of Shaphat of Abel Meholah you shall anoint [as] prophet in your place. It shall be [that] whoever escapes the sword of Hazael, Jehu will kill; and whoever escapes the sword of Jehu, Elisha will kill.

Look at the assignment God gave to Elijah. Three names are mentioned in the Scriptures above. Between 1 Kings 19 and 2 Kings 9, we did not hear anything about Hazael and Jehu. Something happened to their lives. Remember, God.s instruction is that Elijah should anoint three men, but as he was going, he found Elisha.

The question is this: why did he not find Jehu? How come he didn.t locate Hazael? What is their problem? Where were they when Elijah found Elisha? From that 1 Kings 19 to 2 Kings 9, Elisha did not stop following Elijah.

Before 2 Kings 9, Elisha was called Elisha the Tishbite. But in 2 Kings 9:1, he was called Elisha the prophet. He had manifested after thirteen years of following Elijah. Elijah died without anointing Jehu. Elisha took over. You can decide you will manifest in the next 55 years or you can decide you will start to manifest now.

Jehu was supposed to be king over Israel. He had an assignment to avenge the death of Naboth (1 Kings 21:1-19). God had said dogs will lick the blood of Jezebel on the same land where she and her husband, Ahab, had connived to kill Naboth. Many years had passed and the man who had been foretold will do this had not done it.

So, Elisha woke up one day, grabbed his bottle of oil and asked his servant to go and anoint him. If you read 2 Kings 9 very well, the servant was specifically instructed to draw Jehu away from amongst his friends and anoint him in the house. He was even instructed to anoint him and run away. This man Jehu had to be forcefully anointed because he seemed absolutely unready. A man who was supposed to be king was busy playing among complacent people.

Immediately the oil came upon Jehu, he came to himself. Leaving that place, he went on his assignment and he killed everybody that God said he would kill. He went to fulfill his assignment, but for how long did the world had to wait? He had the potential to do it but he was sleeping. Jehu was sleeping until somebody had to help him. Until kingship was forced upon him, he was unready.

I read a funny comic on Facebook some time ago. It reads this: I hereby apply for the post of security man in your company, but I have caught you this time around. Every time I apply, you will say, .No vacancy.. This time, I have caught you red-handed. The security man you had before has died. I even attended his burial. You cannot tell me now that there is no vacancy. Let me see how you will tell me that there is no vacancy. The writer was ready to take it by force.

Until Elisha went to meet Jehu, Jehu did not carry out all the exploits he was supposed to. If Elisha had not taken that step to anoint Jehu, perhaps Jehu would have died without fulfilling the purpose of God. The world is expecting the manifestation of the sons of God. The world is expecting your manifestation.

Look at the story of the three men. It was in chapter 8 of second King that Hazael also became the king of Syria. It was even Elisha that sent a prophecy to him (See 2 Kings 8:7-13).

There are reasons why Elisha did not miss his time. Let.s look at those reasons:

1.   Elisha was at the right place at the

right time.

There is the place of positioning in destiny. Many Christians are not manifesting because they are not in the right place. They are in the wrong location for their lives. The Bible says in Genesis 2:8 that God planted a garden eastward in Eden, and there He put the man whom He had formed. There was a place where God expected Adam to be, and that was where all his provisions had been made for him. The next time God looked in that place and Adam was not there, he missed God.s original design for his life.

In the same way, God.s provision can only reach a man where Providence expects him to be. This is why I am often surprised at people who are always so eager to leave one state for another in a bid to find greener pastures (which is not bad, by the way), but you have to be sure it is God.s will that you should even relocate to a particular place. If there is a prayer you need to pray always, it is that, God, let me always be at the right place at the right time.

In a church one day, God opened the eyes of the servant of God to see an angel. The angel had brought three babies, in answer to the prayer of those who were praying for the fruit of the womb. The day the babies were brought, most of the church members were not in attendance. Do you know that they could pray for another twenty years and they will never have those children again?

In one of the miracles of Jesus, the man by the pool of Bethesda mentioned that the angel comes once to stir the water; whoever is available at that time gets the healing (See John 5:2-9). You have to be at the right place at the right time. Your location may just be too unhelpful for you to manifest. Elisha was at the right place at the right time. This talks about right positioning.

How Can You Always Be Rightly Positioned?

The company that a man keeps is very significant in his journey towards destiny fulfillment. If you are always in the company of wrong people people who aren.t going anywhere you are already badly positioned. If you are often concerned about mixing with people who do not consider sin to be a serious issue or people who joke with God.s instructions, you are already pushing yourself out of your divine location. Staying within God.s instructions is a prerequisite to maintaining the right position. God.s best will always find you when you are within His instructions and commandments.

Ps. 1:1-3 reads:

> **Blessed [is] the man Who walks not in the counsel of the ungodly, Nor stands in the path of sinners, Nor sits in the seat of the scornful; 2But his delight [is] in the law of the LORD, And in His law he meditates day and night. 3He shall be like a tree Planted by the rivers of water, That brings forth its fruit in its season, Whose leaf also shall not wither; And whatever he does shall prosper.**

That means there is a place you can be and you will not be blessed. Blessed is the man who sits not, stands not, or walks not in the ways of sinners. There are people who stand in the way of sinners, no wonder they will not be blessed. A man who stands among wise men shall be wise, but the companion of fools will be destroyed (Prov. 13:20).

2. Elisha was hard working

Elijah found Elisha working. The young man was hard working. Scripture says whatever your hand finds to do, do it with your might (Eccl. 9:10). Many people want to be great but they are not doing anything. Christianity is not a license to be lazy, as some people have wrongly believed.

Even the Holy Spirit speaking through Apostle Paul in 1 Thessalonians 4: 11-12 says,

> **That you also aspire to lead a quiet life, to mind your own business, and to WORK WITH YOUR OWN HANDS, as we commanded you, that you may walk properly toward those who**

**are outside, and [that] you
may lack nothing.**

Did you read that? The Bible says you must
work with your own hands so that you may
not embarrass Jesus before unbelievers due
to laziness and so that you will not lack
anything.

Prayer does not give you the license to be
lazy. You should pray as you work and you
must work diligently as you pray. Both must
go hand in hand. Deuteronomy 28:12 says:

> **"The LORD will open to you
> His good treasure, the
> heavens, to give the rain to
> your land in its season, and
> to bless all the work of your
> hand. You shall lend to
> many nations, but you shall
> not borrow.**

He will bless all the work that is in your
hands. If there is no work in your hands, He
has nothing to bless. Can you please look
for something to do?

So many people have prayed so many prayers. They even have month long vigils and mountain visitations because of this. I guess they are praying because they do not have work to do. They are praying for God to do something, yet they do not have any work to do. God can do nothing if you have nothing in your hands. God will only bless the work that is in your hands. So when there is no work in your hands, you can pray till eternity and nothing will happen. If you are not vigorously invested in your work, God has nothing to bless.

Elisha was hard working. He was plowing. In fact, to prove how hard working he was, he said, Give me time to hand over my work (See 1 Kings 19:19-20). It sounded like, I have decided I am going to do this work of ministry that I have been called into, but I need to make sure that this secular business is properly handed over to someone who can take over.

Take a look at all the disciples that Jesus called, they were working. Matthew was at his tax collecting booth when Jesus called him. John, Peter, and Andrew were all fishing when Jesus called them. Jesus met them doing their work. So He cannot come and take their work from them only to give them what will not pay. No wonder they asked Him, What will be our reward for following you? He not only assured them of reward in heaven, He also assured them of reward here on earth.

Elisha was hard working. He was a man given to labour. The hand of the diligent will rule, but the lazy man will be put to forced labor (Proverbs 12:24). What is rulership? Rulership is manifestation. Manifestation can only be preceded by diligence. The hand of the diligent person will bear fruit.

You may be thinking, I need capital to do my work, but do you know that you can start somewhere? Tell God, I have looked for what to do but cannot find. Please bless this one that my hand has found. Back in the day, water was sold in cheap nylons. Then later, someone thought of making it into sachet water. Before we knew it, sachet water has taken over the country.

If you are genuine and you say, This is what I have, and you work with it, you will be blessed. A lazy man deserves to be hungry. The man who does not provide for his household is worse than an infidel (1 Tim. 5:8).

This does not exclude women also. If anyone does not work and is reluctant to work, he should not eat and he deserves to be hungry.

The one who will not provide for his household is worse than an unbeliever. God knows that there could be reasons for this, but He is not approving of those reasons. If God says if you do not work you should not eat, then you can go to Him and say, God I want to work and this is what I want to do. Please bless the work of my hands. God will bless it because He said that the whole world is waiting for the manifestation of the sons of God (Rom 8:19).

If you are a son of God, you have a destiny to manifest. You carry a mandate to manifest. It is God.s mandate. The Bible says none of God.s word will go without being fulfilled. It is God.s mandate. Therefore, He is committed to it. If He says it, He will make it work.

3. Elisha was prepared to learn the way and pay the price of his calling

The Bible says Elisha began to serve Elijah from the day he was anointed (1 Kings 19:21). For the next thirteen years, he was learning the trade of the ministry he had received. There was need for servanthood before he could be manifested. No wonder Jesus said, he who must lead must first serve (Mark 9:35). Elisha learned the role, no wonder he became great.

Even when it was time for Elijah to depart, Elisha.s service to Elijah was so strong that amongst all the sons of the prophets, only Elisha followed Elijah until he was taken away, and this kind of followership granted Elisha double portion of Elijah.s anointing.

Sometimes, I marvel at how we grapple desperately for the first position. I wonder at how we are quick to quickly put down our names to serve in church, but when it really comes down to it, only few people go all the way to be committed to serve. You cannot be a good leader if you are not a great follower. You cannot lead if you don.t learn to follow.

By its meaning alone, manifestation shows that something was initially in the dark before it came into the light; something was initially unknown before it became known. We do not know how long it took for it to become known, but we know it stayed through its training period and soon became known.

Jesus. ministry lasted for only three and half years, but He had to prepare for it for thirty years. Such lengthy preparation can almost not work in our day and age where so many people (especially young people) want to get rich quick. Very few people want to be subordinates; only few want to serve their way to the top.

But we see that Elisha served his way to the top. Perhaps you do not know that Elisha had a thriving business (1 Kings 19:19). He was a rich man, because when he was about to start following Elijah, he had to kill a yoke of oxen and make a feast for his departure (1 Kings 19:21). This proves to us that he was not a hireling; he was the owner of his business. But he was willing to be taken away to learn under somebody so that he can become the man he was originally created to be. At the end of his life, he achieved such a great feat that years later, his dead, dried bones raised a dead man (2 Kings 13:21).

Are you willing to serve your way to the top? Are you willing to learn all you need now to become all that you were made to be? You may need to serve faithfully as a subordinate under a tyrannical leader in that office. You just serve faithfully. You may need to just be a faithful worker in your church; where other workers are joking with God.s work, coming in anytime they like, you will choose to be faithful. You may need to decide you will only do what Jesus would do no matter what it will cost you. In the end, what will result is that God will honour you. God always does.

You may need to go back to school. You

may have to learn new skills. You may need to improve your present skill, knowledge, or sharpen your talent. Someone said, You can.t get paid beyond how much you are worth. If what you can do with your skill is what every other Tom and Jones can do, then you cannot be more successful than them. You must mark yourself out of the status quo. You must be willing to learn and serve before you can manifest.

Let.s now compare the life of Jehu and what ruled him out from not manifesting on time.

1. Jehu was in the wrong company.
Jehu was in the company of people who didn.t know where they were going. Reading 2 Kings 9:4-5, you will find that Jehu was an army commander and he was sitting with some of the captains, but these weren.t the people he was supposed to be sitting with. Destiny was waiting for him somewhere else and he was busy here with people he was supposed to be ruling over and commanding.

The greatest harm you can do to yourself is

to be in the wrong company. Your company defines who you are. It has been said that if you are better than eight people amongst your ten friends, then you are in the wrong company. If you are better than at least two people amongst your ten friends, then you are in the right company; such company will help you become better and will keep leading you to heights that are greater than you.

If you want to manifest, you must check your company. Who are the people in your company? Birds of the same feathers flock together. A foolish friend cannot make you any wiser.

Who are your friends? What is their motivation? What is their inspiration? You can easily look forward to those who are better than you to inspire you to move forward.

Jehu was with the wrong people. He was perpetually in the company of men who do not share the same vision or aspiration with him. He that walks with the wise shall be wise. The people you walk with speak a lot about where you will end up.

2. Jehu was unmotivated

Another major problem with Jehu, which I have found to be a problem in the body of Christ, is that Jehu was too casual. He was ordinary. He was not moved. He was unmotivated. The fact that he had a mandate and the power of God upon his life and he is not coming to manifestation does not mean anything to him. Where David said, the zeal of the LORD.s house has consumed me, Jehu was too cold, even about spiritual matters. If things are working, fine, so be it. And if things are not working, for Jehu, it is just as it should be.

This was why the servant was instructed to take Jehu into to inner chamber before he was anointed. This means that he needed a deeper experience. He needed a one-on-one encounter with God.

The problem with most of us is that we only take cursory looks but never pay critical attention to the matter we are supposed to. If you look at that situation critically, you can come to conclusion that there is something wrong somewhere and you need to fix it. Only then can you realize where you missed it, what wrong step you took, whom you walked with that you shouldn.t have walked with, what you did wrong.

Immediately Jehu was anointed, he got the fire to fulfill his destiny. When he casually announced to his friends that the young servant had come to anoint him king, his friends fell on their faces to acknowledge his kingship. This means that if he had manifested before now, no one would have refused his leadership. It is because he did not take steps, that he remained where he was. The moment he decided to take step, he was acknowledged.

The prodigal son.s mistake was not that he asked for his belonging. No, it is not. The father would not have given him if it was abnormal. He demanded for his own portion of the inheritance and after collecting his portion, he went to a far country. Going to the far country was not his problem. If he had gone to the far country and had done business with his inheritance, he probably would have been more successfully. His problem was that he squandered his wealth. He mismanaged what he had collected.

When the prodigal son returned and the elder brother complained about him, that his father never killed a fowl for him since he had been living in the house with him, the father.s response was shocking. The father said, All that I have is yours (Luke 15:31). That means the whole time, this elder brother had all things from his father and yet never asked, and this younger son was smart enough to ask, though he wasted it.

The responsibility to rise depends on you. The responsibility to manifest lies in your hands. Look at Elisha and Jehu, whose example do you want to follow? Elijah was supposed to meet with three men, but he met only Elisha. The other people were nowhere to be found. If they had been at the right place, if they had been hardworking, if they had been with the right company, perhaps they would have been found early and they would have manifested early.

Don.t be cut unawares. You can take charge of your life starting today and start actualizing all of God.s blessings and victories for you. You can start to take advantage of your God-given privileges to begin to shine forth. This place where you are now is your place of rest. You are long overdue for manifestation. Will you begin today to manifest?

Chapter Three

OVERCOMING CHALLENGES

TO MANIFESTATION

For the vision [is] yet for an
appointed time; but at the end it
will speak, and it will not lie.
Though it tarries, wait for it;
because it will surely come, it
will not tarry. Hab. 2:3

As we have considered in the previous
chapter, manifestation can be
delayed. The promise of greatness
can tarry. There is no doubt that there are
challenges in the world. These challenges are

simply inevitable. While we may have analyzed the lives of Elisha and Jehu in the previous chapter, comparing and contrasting their lives relative to how they both manifested, some of the delays to manifestation may not be self-inflicted.

Sometimes we try all we can to make things fall into place, but challenges come in the way and those plans become thwarted. It is a popular saying that he who fail to prepare will always inevitably fail. If you do not know your life (even as a Christian) won.t always be a bed of roses, you would always expect a smooth sail through life.

There is an area in Ibadan, Nigeria called Challenge. One of the days, the Managing Director of my former place of work mentioned that some staff of the company.s branch in that area often complain that they are not doing well. The MD replied jokingly, They will not do well since the area is called Challenge. The name should instead be changed to Lagos Ibadan Bypass, he said. People are often wary of challenges, and this is because challenges are constant in life.

Hebrews 12: 1-2 reads:

> Therefore we also, since we are surrounded by so great a cloud of witnesses, let us lay aside every weight, and the sin which so easily ensnares [us,] and let us run with endurance the race that is set before us, looking unto Jesus, the author and finisher of [our] faith, who for the joy that was set before Him endured the cross, despising the shame, and has sat down at the right hand of the throne of God.

Jesus Christ faced His own challenges. The Scripture above says He endured the cross and He despised the shame. To endure a thing is to bear with it, even though you would rather wish it wasn.t happening. If Jesus endured it, then it means it wasn.t palatable. At some point, He said, God, I wish that this cup will pass over Me. I wish I don.t have to go this way. I wish there is an easier road to fulfill this commandment, but nevertheless, Your will be done (Emphasis mine).

It was tough to follow through with God.s commandment. He was in the middle of one of the direst moments of his life. The temptation in the wilderness for forty days was a far cry compared to this period of His life. In few hours, He would have to decide whether to go through with God.s demand His crucifixion or whether to compromise and give up. Mind you, if He had given up and told the Father He couldn.t go along with it, it would have been the first rejection of God.s will in His 33 years of living. But praise God Jesus didn.t quit on you and me.

The Bible says Jesus Christ learned obedience by the things He suffered (Heb. 5:8). He stepped into glory by going through every single thing God wanted Him to go through. He could never be glorified unless He suffered everything He did. Hebrews says He became qualified to become our High Priest because He was tested in every way and yet He did not give in, and in that Jesus was tested in every way, He is able to help those who are tested (Heb.

2:17-18). This means that because Jesus suffered terribly before He manifested, He is able to help those who suffer also on their way to manifesting.

Hebrews 2:17-18 reads:

Therefore, in all things He had to be made like [His] brethren, that He might be a merciful and faithful High Priest in things [pertaining] to God, to make propitiation for the sins of the people. For in that He Himself has suffered, being tempted, He is able to aid those who are tempted.

By this Scripture alone, we can conclude that challenges are qualifications for manifestation. If a man must manifest, the road must be fraught by challenges. Those challenges are not there to push you out of the road. They are not intended to stop you from manifesting. Actually, they are there to examine those who are serious and those who are not serious about manifesting. Those challenges want to know how serious you are about showing forth. This is the reason why only few people qualify to manifest, because very few people determine to push through to the end.

Judges 7:5-7 reads:

> So he brought the people down to the water. And the Lord said to Gideon, Everyone who laps from the water with his tongue, as a dog laps, you shall set apart by himself; likewise everyone who gets down on his knees to drink. And the number of those who lapped, putting their hand to their mouth, was three hundred men; but all the rest of the people got down on their knees to drink water. Then the Lord said to Gideon, .By the three hundred men who lapped I will save you, and deliver the Midianites into your hand. Let all the other people go, every man to his place.

In the above scripture, a total number of Thirty two thousand (32,000) men set out to be enlisted to the Israel Army under the leadership of Gideon to go to war with the very powerful Midianites. They wanted to be among the Victorious Army of God that will bring victory to Israel from their age long oppressors, the Midianites. But alas, after being subjected to true test of their strength and what it takes to manifest, only three hundred (300) of them qualified and they went ahead to manifest as the Lord brought victory for the Israelites through them. Indeed, most times, only few do succeed to manifest as many people are usually not ready to pay the price for their manifestation. The question is, Will you be among the few that will lap water with their tongue?

So many people can say something about so many things, but when it finally comes down to it, they cannot stay through the tide of tests. When the barrage of the first tests comes, they will fall flat on their faces and will ask to bail out. Such people are cut short from manifesting.

Manifestation is not going to come easy. Nobody said it would. Jesus Christ, our Mediator, suffered outside of the gate (Heb. 13:12). He was humiliated and badly beaten. He was scourged and mocked. There is nothing as pitiful as having over 600 soldiers spit on you, but go and read your Bible very well, Jesus Christ was spat upon by this number of soldiers. When He should have been allowed to take a shorter route to Golgotha where He would be crucified, the soldiers took him through a longer route so that He can be monumentally disgraced.

If you have been expecting a shorter route to manifestation, there is no use seeking to manifest. There is no shorter route. Most people who have been looking for the easy way to get rich or become famous have found themselves selling their souls to the devil. Some may not have done it literally, but as far as the Kingdom of God is concerned, they have bowed themselves to the devil, betrayed the Lord Jesus Who saved them, and are not worthy to be called sons of God. They may have all the affluence and fame, but heaven has no record of them in their books whatsoever.

The truth is that challenges are difficult. They are tunnels you wish you could circumvent. They are barriers you wish would not be on your way to greatness. If there was a straight road to manifestation that didn.t cost your soul, you would take it. But unfortunately, there is no such road. Jesus faced His own challenges. You will have to face the same on your way to manifesting. They are inevitable.
What are they things you should know about challenges?

1. God is aware that we face challenges

God is not oblivious that you are passing through challenges or that you will pass through challenges. God is very much aware that you will pass through challenges. James 1:2 says you should count it all joy when you fall into various trials. God knows that there will come times when you will fall into circumstances that are beyond your control.

There comes times when you will look out

the window and everywhere will appear dark. There will be those periods when you would feel you are all alone and nobody is with you again. God is aware of those times. He is not shaken by them and He is not moved or confused by them.

His word says, Can a woman forget her nursing child, and not have compassion on the son of her womb? Surely they may forget, yet I will not forget you (Isaiah 49:15).

Matthew 7:7-11 reads:
>**"Ask, and it will be given to you; seek, and you will find; knock, and it will be opened to you. For everyone who asks receives, and he who seeks finds, and to him who knocks it will be opened. Or what man is there among you who, if his son asks for bread, will give him a stone? Or if he asks for a fish, will he give him a serpent? If you then, being evil, know how to give good gifts to your**

children, how much more will your Father who is in heaven give good things to those who ask Him!

God knows and understands what you are passing through. God knows that at some points in your life, it would look as if everything is over for you. God is fully aware of the wiles of devil and that he would seek to destroy your destiny.

Let.s read John 16:33:

"These things I have spoken to you, that in Me you may have peace. In the world you will have tribulation; but be of good cheer, I have overcome the world."

According to the scripture, when God looks for you and He realizes you are in the world, He expects that you would face challenges. He expects that storms would come. But He encourages you to be of good cheer because he has defeated the world for you. He has conquered the devil for your sake. He didn.t have to raise His hand at the devil, but He did, and He did so for your sake. Praise the Lord!

God is aware that there are times when it will look like nothing is working for you. God is aware. So stay calm in His love.

2. God did not promise us a problem-free life

No place in the Scriptures did God assure us that since you have come to Him, you will have a problem-free life. He did not promise us that. If God had promised that, then there would be no need for us to wait for the coming of Jesus the second time. The world would have become our utopia.

Isaiah 43:1-3 reads:

> **But now, thus says the LORD, who created you, O Jacob, And He who formed you, O Israel: "Fear not, for I have redeemed you; I have called [you] by your name; You [are] Mine. When you pass through the waters, I [will be] with you; And**

through the rivers, they shall not overflow you. When you walk through the fire, you shall not be burned, Nor shall the flame scorch you. For I [am] the LORD your God, The Holy One of Israel, your Savior; I gave Egypt for your ransom, Ethiopia and Seba in your place.

From the Scripture above, God did not say, If you pass through fire, but rather When you pass through It is not a conditional statement. It is a matter that is bound to occur. That means it is certain that you will pass through storms. When talks about the time it would occur, although you do not know what time or day or month it would occur.

Many believers have been wrongly taught to think that when you come into Jesus Christ and you give your life to Him, you will have a trouble-free life. This is not true. Absolutely not true.

On the contrary, the life in Jesus brings more challenges than the life outside of Him, because we are in the world that does not readily applaud holy living and separation from unrighteousness, which is a serious standard in Christianity (John 15:18-19, 1 John 3:13).

God is not afraid of your problems. In fact, the more the problem, the more the glory. This is because God takes a special concern in showing forth His glory in His children to disgrace the devil. But oftentimes, we have disgraced God by misbehaving in the middle of challenges, by not trusting God wholly for victory.

We serve a God who uses egg to break palm kernel, just to disgrace the stone. In the real sense, is this possible? No, it isn.t. But this is the kind of God we serve. He is a Father Who takes delight in working in greatly mysteriously ways such that it surprises us and it shocks the devil.

When God raised ordinary Joseph to become a prime minister in a strange country, the devil was shocked. His brothers who never imagined his boastful dreams would come to pass saw live how God could turn evil to good.

What others meant for evil, God used for good. God chooses the foolishness of this world to confound the wisdom of the wise (1 Cor. 1:27). He chooses the feeble things to disgrace the strong. This is the God you serve.

So God did not promise you trouble-free, tribulation-free, challenge-free life, because if God had promised such, you would say God is unfaithful for bringing certain circumstances your way. But God is always faithful to you, no matter what (1 Cor. 10:13, Jer. 31:3). If He did not tell you something, then you should not expect it; but if He told you challenges will come, then you should expect it and know that God Who promised it will also defend you.

We have a great assurance through Apostle Paul in 1 Corinthians 10:13 which reads:

No temptation has overtaken you except such as

is common to man; but God is faithful, who will not allow you to be tempted beyond what you are able, but with the temptation will also make a way of escape, that you may be able to bear it

You will overcome every challenge in Him.

3. You are never alone in your challenges. God is always with you.

Hebrews 13:5 reads:

[Let your] conduct [be] without covetousness; [be] content with such things as you have. For He Himself has said, "I WILL NEVER LEAVE YOU NOR FORSAKE YOU.

The Amplified translation of that Scripture reads:

Let your character or moral disposition be free from

love of money [including greed, avarice, lust, and craving for earthly possessions] and be satisfied with your present [circumstances and with what you have]; for He [God] Himself has said, I will not in any way fail you nor give you up nor leave you without support. [I WILL] NOT, [I WILL] NOT, [I WILL] NOT IN ANY DEGREE LEAVE YOU HELPLESS NOR FORSAKE NOR LET [YOU] DOWN (RELAX MY HOLD ON YOU)! [ASSUREDLY NOT!].

In the face of the most heated challenge, God is always there with you. This is what God has promised. I think one of the greatest promises of God is that He is faithful (1 Cor. 10:13). Faithful means constantly committed.

This means that no matter what comes your

way, God is constantly committed to you; like a faithful husband who will never leave his wife alone, God is your Husband Who will never cheat on you, nor will He leave you one second. Scriptures even say that His eyes are always on you (Ps. 139:7-10). How more assuring can that be!

The three Hebrews were told they would be thrown into the fire, but they replied, Hear ye, oh king. We know our God whom we serve shall deliver us. And even if He does not deliver us, we still will not bow down to your image (Dan 3:16-18). The Bible says, they threw them into the fire and the fire was so greatly heated that the heat of the fire killed the people who threw them into the fire.

Listen, what a child of the devil goes through that burns him will only serve to soothe the child of God. What threatens the child of the devil and even bring him death may threaten God.s child but will never overcome him. The same Hebrew boys who were thrown into the furnace were not killed, though those who threw them into the fire died from the same hotness of the fire. The three Hebrew boys had it tougher because they were thrown directly into the fire.

No matter what you are going through, no matter how it seem you do not deserve it because an unbeliever around you isn.t going through the same, cheer up because you will always, always come out better.

2 Corinthians 4:17 reads:
For our light affliction, which is but for a moment, is working for us a far more exceeding [and] eternal weight of glory.

The king was coming towards the fire to announce their obituary. He was coming to confirm that they were totally burnt up. But he got the shock of his life when he noticed these same people were not burned and that someone like the son of God was there with them.

God will not send someone to help you when you are in the fire; He comes Himself to rescue you. God doesn.t stop the fire before He gets there. No. When they are building the fire for you, God doesn.t put it out. God allows you to enter into the fire. But the good thing is that any time you are in the fire, God Himself shows up to quench the fire.

The fire did not die out but the Hebrew boys were inside the fire. The Bible says their clothes were not touched. They had not even smoke smell on them. Their bodies did not change. They were not roasted. It was like being in an air-conditioned room. God takes glory in being with you in the fire, and in you realizing He is with you in the fire.

Daniel was thrown to the lions and it seemed the lions were on holiday. They were suddenly on a compulsory fast. God has promised that when you are in trouble, He will help you; and because He is a faithful Father, He will always show up to help you (Heb. 10:35-38).

He wants you to manifest in every area of your life, because it is His will that you manifest (3 John 1:2). Whatever the devil may be trying with you, God is always with you to fight for you. You have to believe it and take a stand for it in faith (John 10:10; John 11:25-26; 1 John 5:4; 2 Cor. 5:7; Heb. 10:38).

4. You need to confront your challenges with spiritual weapons.

Ephesians 6:12:

> **For we do not wrestle against flesh and blood, but against principalities, against powers, against the rulers of the darkness of this age, against spiritual [hosts] of wickedness in the heavenly [places.]**

If you go into battle with the wrong weapon, you will certainly be defeated. If you are supposed to be fighting the enemy with artillery weapon and you are using pistol, he will defeat you. I remember a movie where there was supposed to be a fight between a cowboy and a kungfu fighter.

The kungfu fighter was making fierce-looking kungfu gestures and was running towards the cowboy. The cowboy, undaunted, just simply pulled out his pistol and shot once. The kungfu fighter dropped dead. He had brought the wrong weapon to fight his enemy.

If you bring the wrong weapon to fight your challenges, you will always lose. If at your office, there is a superior who is threatening you and trying all manner of wicked ways to just get you out of the company, your action shouldn.t be to retaliate physically, your action should be to report him to your Father.

Get on your knees and pray about the issue, whatever the issue may be. The strength of a Christian is in his relationship with God. What makes you strong is your relationship with God. you have God on speed dial and you can talk to Him about everything; absolutely everything.

The Scripture we read here says we are not battling with human enemies, but devils and demons. Does this mean they come to us physically or always in our dreams? No.

Devils can take over human beings and so begin to manipulate them to attack you. This is why you must always put on the whole armour of God all the time as a Christian. This is what guarantees your constant victory over every challenge. This is how you win any battle on your way to manifestation.

If you come to your battle with your head unguarded, the enemy will target that area. Whichever area of your body is exposed during battle is a major area the enemy can attack you. Ephesians 6:13-17 reads:

> Therefore TAKE UP THE WHOLE ARMOR OF GOD, that you may be able to withstand in the evil day, and having done all, to stand. Stand therefore, having girded your waist with truth, having put on the breastplate of righteousness, and having shod your feet with the preparation of the gospel of peace; above all, taking the

shield of faith with which you will be able to quench all the fiery darts of the wicked one. And take the helmet of salvation, and the sword of the Spirit, which is the word of God.

What the above scripture means is that you should fight in the place of prayer, using the weapon of the Word of God, and absolute dependence upon God. Put on the helmet of salvation means that you should think like a child of God, a saved person; not an unbeliever. God loves you and should never think anything less than that.

Hold up the shield of faith by standing constantly and permanently upon the word of God no matter how tough the situation. You will only be able to quench the fiery darts of the enemy, which are doubts and unbelief, when you stand alone upon God.s word and His promises to you. The devil only needs you to get outside of God.s word before he can defeat you.

Gird yourself with the belt of truth means

that you believe only and live by the truth that Jesus taught and lived (2 John 1:9-11). Anything besides what Jesus Christ taught and lived is not the truth and you should not believe it (John 14:6; Acts 1:1; Prov. 30:5).

Put on the breastplate of righteousness by ensuring that you are constantly living like a Christian and your life is free of blame (1 John 2:6; 2 Cor. 10:6; 1 Cor. 11:31). As long as your life is blameless, the enemy has nothing to hold to and God has the right of way to work out your victory smoothly.

Shod your feet with the preparation of the gospel of peace simply means that you should always be ready to let others know about your Jesus (1 Tim. 2:3-4; 2 Tim. 2:2). If He is sweet and real to you, you will talk about Him.

Wield the sword of the Spirit, which is the Word of God, by studying to show yourself approved unto God (2 Tim. 2:15). The more of God.s word you know and understand and are practicing, the more victory is constantly assured for you. Ignorance is the devil.s greatest weapon to relieving Christians of their God.s given rights. When your life is soaked in the word, the devil can never take advantage of you (Deut. 30:20; Ps. 119:165; Ps 119:11).

This is the exact armour you need to wear to fight every battle you face on your way to manifesting. You are not going to fight in your own strength. Your weapon is in God, and God has guaranteed you constant victory if you fight with the right weapon.

5.   God.s grace is available for you

1 Corinthians 10:13 reads:

No temptation has overtaken you except such as is common to man; but God [is] faithful, who will not allow you to be tempted beyond what you are able, but with the temptation will also make the way of escape, that you may be able to bear [it.]

God will never allow you to be tempted beyond what you can bear. But the good news is that even in the temptation, He will make a way of escape. 2 Corinthian 12:9:

> **And He said to me, "My grace is sufficient for you, for My strength is made perfect in weakness." Therefore most gladly I will rather boast in my infirmities, that the power of Christ may rest upon me.**

Paul begged God to stop this issue, but God would rather have him go inside the problem so that He can show him He can save him inside the problem.

If Jesus Christ had gone to Bethany before the death of Lazarus, the glory of God wouldn.t have been greatly manifested in the resurrection of Lazarus. When He was called to come while Lazarus was still sick, He refused to come.

In fact, Jesus Himself knew Lazarus was dead four days before He went to wake Him up. He waited for the man to die and be dead for four days before He went to raise him up. He proved to them that He did not only have the power to stop people from dying, but He had the power to raise them back to life again.

Oftentimes, God will only show up at the peak of the challenge so that all glory will be ascribed to Him. Your faith will be strengthened when you see how miraculously He showed up for you when you least expected, and so that men may marvel at the magnificence of God.

Throughout the periods of those challenges, God has promised that His grace His ability where you need it, when you need it, to the extent that you need it is available for you. You may feel you are too weak to fight through the challenges, but God says His grace will carry you through.

Some people think it would have been so good if God had answered on time. Actually, God cannot be too late. He is always on time. He has the power to bring back to life. Lazarus had been dead four days. He was stinking. He was smelling. The people believed that if Jesus had come before He died, Lazarus would have lived. Yet Jesus said, No, I can show you that I have power over life and over death. And death heard His voice and it gave up the dead in it.

The grace of God is always available. In every situation, God.s grace is sufficient for you. That settles the matter. The reason why God allowed you to pass through all these up to this time is because He wants to show you greater glory.

The glory of bringing Lazarus from the dead is greater than the glory of stopping him from dying. The glory of raising him after four days in the grave is greater than the glory of raising him immediately he died. That way, people could have assumed Lazarus was probably partially dead and so it was easy for Jesus to bring him back to life.

They asked Jesus Christ, Who sinned, this man or his parents, that he should be born blind? He was called a man. He was not a boy. He was not a baby. It means from the very first day he was born into the world, he was born blind, and he grew up into a man still blind. Before the Bible could refer to him as a man, he must be above thirty years. Jesus Christ replied, Neither this man nor his parents, but that the glory of God should be revealed in him. No wonder the man.s miracle created controversy.

A great miracle usually would create controversy. No one will be able to trace it to anybody what God will do for you. Grace is God working the ability and willingness in you to do what He wants you to do so that you can manifest (Phil. 2:13). Stay within God.s grace which is sufficient for you.

6. Every problem has an expiry date

> But may the God of all grace, who called us to His eternal glory by Christ Jesus, after you have suffered a while, perfect, establish, strengthen, and settle [you.] 1 Pet. 5:10:

The world has a beginning and the world

has an end. Every movie, no matter how long, will always come to an end. Every examination will always have a final paper. In the same way, every challenge will always have an expiration date. You will not die in that problem. Jesus will always work a way out for you.

Remember Peter and his crew when they were fishing. They had toiled all night and had caught nothing. It seemed like they had worked futilely, because in truth, that was the reality. But when Jesus stepped into the situation, He only spoke a word. As soon as Peter obeyed, they caught so many fishes the Bible says their boat was almost sinking.

One would have taught Noah was foolish to be the only man on earth who believed water will fall from the sky. At this time, the world did not know rain; water irrigated the earth from under the ground. But a man, who claimed to have heard God, was foolishly building a boat because he said his God was going to destroy the earth with flood from the sky. It was a period of shame for Noah.

His family even had to mock him. But his faith in God was steadfast and as he kept building the ark, he knew that one day, all that God said would come to pass; and so it did.

All of a sudden, water started to pour from the sky and it didn.t stop until after forty days and forty nights. The man who believed the impossible had experienced the miraculous. If you will just believe the impossible, God will show you the miraculous. You will laugh your way to victory because you will realize then that God is truly faithful to you.

Most of the glorious hymns of thanksgiving came from men and women who had touched God.s miracle and couldn.t hold back. They just had to burst forth into songs and so they penned down some of the oldest but powerful hymns ever. When the LORD gives you the victory you have always envisaged, you will dance and sing new songs.

God, Whom you serve in truth and in spirit, promises that the problem will expire soon.

God only wants to use this challenge to improve your faith and bolster your patience, so that you can be able to managed appropriately the manifestation that will happen to you in the coming level (Jas. 1:2-4).

Chapter Four

PROSPERING BY THE LORD

Thus says the LORD, your
Redeemer, The Holy One of
Israel: "I [am] the LORD your
God, Who teaches you to profit,
Who leads you by the way you
should go. Isa. 48:17

One of the characteristics of
manifestation is good news. By good
news, I refer to prospering, and this
prosperity is caused by the Lord. The Bible
says the blessing of the Lord is what makes
us rich and God adds no sorrow to this kind

of prosperity (Prov. 10:22). God.s riches upon a man.s life removes sorrow from his life or is absolutely lacking in sorrow.

You may have heard that most rich people in the world are often plagued by one disease or the other, and also that they have a hard time enjoying those riches because they constantly have sleepless nights or lawsuits to battle with. God removes all those from His children.

When God blesses you, He blesses you perfectly. You will be rich in wealth and also be rich in health. You will be rich in your cognitive ability and also be rich in security, because the LORD your God protects and guards you. Your children will be healthy. Your spouse will be strong. Your in-laws will love and favour you. You will always hear good news.

I do not mean that things will always be perfect and trouble-free. I do not mean that there won.t be enemies wishing to throw you down. When your way pleases God, He makes even your enemies to be at peace with you (Prov 16:7).

There may be little troubles here and there, but God will always be there to give you peace. What agitates the unbelievers will never agitate you, because God has given you peace on every side (1 Kings 4:22-24; 1 Kings 5:4; John 14:27). That is the kind of prosperity God gives to His children. Psalm 91 is a proof of all these.

Have you read the Scripture that says God is able to do exceedingly abundantly above all that we ask or think (Eph. 3:20)? It means that God takes what you ask for and goes beyond what you ask to give you even what you did not ask for. In the case of Solomon the king, God asked him to make a single request. Because the man made a request that pleased God so much, God not only granted him that request, He also gave him far much more than he (Solomon) could imagine (1 Kings 3:11-13).

You may wonder why manifestation isn.t only limited to spiritual maturity and advancement in the things of God. This is because God wishes for His children to prosper and be in good health as their spirit man prospers (3 John 1:2). This all-round prosperity is required for you not primarily so you can satisfy your own lusts, but so that you may be able to be a blessing to others (1 Thess. 4:11-12; 1 Thess. 5:15).

By your being rich, others can have their needs met. This was how the old church operated. Those who were rich met the needs of those who were poor, and so there was not a single poor person amongst them, because they shared all things in common. Halleluyah! (Acts 2:44; Acts 4:32).

This is why God wants you to prosper.

Manifesting through prosperity is not contrary to God.s will. Our Lord Jesus Christ (Who is equally God) is not averse to it either. Joseph of Arimathea was described as the disciple of Jesus and he was a rich man ((Matt. 27:57; Mark 15:43). Nothing stops you from entering into prosperity so that you can manifest. It is to God.s glory that you manifest.

From this foregoing then, we know that there are some riches that have sorrow with them. Riches that are not a result of God.s blessing will always be backed by sorrows. This is why you see a man who isn.t making progress financially although he is struggling tirelessly to make things work. Yet, there is another man who does less than the former and is tremendously successfully.

This is how the blessing of Lord elevates and separates a man. What the unbelievers struggle with, the man who is blessed by God finds ease in. As the flock of Jacob grew larger and stronger, Laban.s flock grew weaker and thinner. God had visited Jacob and had blessed him; He had withdrawn His blessing from Laban because he was a cheat who constantly took advantage of Jacob (Gen. 30:27-43).

The blessing from the Lord will make a man sleep better. God.s blessing upon a man.s life will give him longer life with good health. The man will be restful and will be hardly diseased from stress or overwork. This kind of riches is devoid of fear of loss. It has absolutely no sorrow included in it.

This is the kind of blessing God wants to give you. In fact, He has reserved it for you in Abraham and you have inherited it already if you are truly in Christ Jesus (Gal. 3:14). You only have to activate it through walking by faith.

This does not mean there will not be challenge at some point in your life. But it means that you will not be seriously shaken. Actually, what makes it easy for you to go through any challenging period at all is because God makes it easy for you; He will never let you be tested beyond what you can bear (1 Cor. 10:13).

He gives you just enough trial to build you up and then He blesses you abundantly in spite of that. Can you see that God is good? In the midst of all the turbulence, you would be relaxed, because God is on your side. The turbulence will bring you greater blessing and glory; challenges are therefore blessings in disguise.

The Man Who Is Truly Blessed
It will not be right to limit this kind of

blessing to money alone. Money is part of it but it is much more than that. The greatest blessing that a Christian has is that he has God. What makes you blessed is the God that you have. If God is always with you, you will always be blessed; whether you have enough money in your bank account or not. You are already a successful man if God is with you (2 Chron. 15:2; Gen. 39:2).

We see this example in the life Joseph when he was in Egypt. The Bible says God was with him and he was a successful man even though he was a slave in the house of his master, Potiphar. Potiphar saw that God was with him because he noticed that whatever he (Joseph) did prospered in his hands (Gen. 39:2-4).

Thus, this means that a man who has God with him will always be blessed. He is the man who is truly blessed. And the sign of this blessing will be that all things will prosper in his hands. Another scripture that proves this is Psalm 1:2-3. Whatsoever the man who delights in God.s word and meditates on it daily does shall prosper. This is why most of the people who believed

God in the scriptures were blessed.

If you are truly serving God and are walking in His ways, you cannot escape being blessed. It is not possible. It is tantamount to saying you are a friend of the Queen of England and you are poor, or have no money to pay your hospital bills, or you are struggling to pay your children.s school fees. Actually, your friendship with her (especially if she loves you dearly) covers all that. How much more God Who loves you much more! (Rom. 8:31-39).

This is how to secure God.s blessing and to prosper: **ALWAYS BE WITH HIM.** If you are always with Him through obeying His word and walking with Him He will always be with you; and if He is always with you, you can be rest assured that you will always be blessed. This blessing is what will teach you how to profit and will show you which way to go (Isa. 48:17; Ps. 32:8).

People will wonder why things work in your hands but they aren.t working in their own hands. Your testimony will be that God is your source and you would have led them to your God just by your testimony of prosperity. Is this not manifestation? Glory to God because this is it.

God Still Prospers People Today

God still prospers people today. Not everyone who is stupendously rich got their riches through dubious means. Nicodemus was a disciple of Jesus Christ and he was one of the Sanhedrin; the elders of Israel. Joseph of Arimathea was a disciple of Jesus Christ and yet he was prosperous.

If you read Matthew 27:57-60 very well, it says that Jesus Christ was buried in a tomb that had never been used; a special tomb provided by this rich Joseph of Arimathea for the same God who had blessed him. God still blesses His children today, and He can bless you, too.

Psalm 34:10 reads,
> **The young lions lack and suffer hunger; But those who seek the Lord shall not lack any good thing.**

The Scripture uses young lions here for a reason. It shows us here that it is the responsibility of the lioness to find food for her cub. But according to the Scripture, there could be circumstances where every effort of the lioness to take care of the cubs fails. Although she is often willing to give food to her cubs, yet she is not always able. But God, Whose children we are, is willing and He is able; therefore, He cannot be incapacitated to take care of us.

There is a popular slogan, the rich also cry. This means that there are times when the strength of the rich man will fail him. The riches of a rich man will fail him. The power of a powerful man will fail him. But the Bible says those who seek the Lord shall not want any good thing. That means there will never be an instance where God failed. God will never be weak. He will never be feeble. He will never be unable or unwilling.

God naturally blesses a man who seeks him (Ps. 84:11). Seeking the Lord automatically qualifies you to have every good thing that you want (Ps. 34:10). The Scriptures here did not say God may give you what you want if you seek Him or you walk uprightly.

No. They blatantly say that God will without fail bless the man who seeks Him; the man who walks uprightly. The man will have his needs met. Is this not prosperity?

All Things Will Always Work For Your Good

Rom. 8:28 reads,

And we know that all things work together for good to those who love God, to those who are the called according to His purpose.

This is my favorite verse in the bible. Every time people ask me what my favorite Bible verse is, I simply quote this verse. This is because when Romans 8:28 is fulfilled in your life, life will be wonderful.

By God.s grace, I am a student of Mathematics. I love mathematics. One of things that, till date, I find so interesting to understand about Mathematics is how negative multiplied by negative equals positive. Two evils become positive, how logical is that?

That is what Romans 8:28 means. Everything works together for your good; no matter how extreme.

When the Lord returned the captivity of Zion, the Bible says we were like them that dreamed (Ps. 126:1). The people themselves could not believe it when the Lord turned the captivity of Zion. If you love God, all things will work together for your good. If you love God, where everyone is receiving a no, you will get a yes.

I remember the first time I went to collect my UK visa years ago. I had been called by the visa office that my visa was ready. I left my office and went to the place. While I was returning to my office, I was too scared to open the wrapped visa in my hand. I was uncertain if it was either positive or negative, and I didn.t want to break down on the road. So I waited till I got to the office. When I did get to the office, I hurried into the convenience and unwrapped the package. As soon as I saw the visa, my heart leaped for joy and I confidently strolled out of the convenience to share the good news with my office colleagues.

God will always make all things work together for your good, because you love Him and you live for Him. What this means in effect is that even the most unpleasant situation that happens to you will turn out in your favor. It would have been unthinkable that a woman like Rahab, a prostitute, will be in the lineage of our Lord Jesus Christ; but she was grafted in because God is able to make all things work together for the good of those who live by faith. Tamar gave birth to children by her father-in-law, Judah, yet she was included into the lineage of our Lord Jesus Christ. These were women whom the world had thought it is over for.

God delights in coming into an inexplicable situation and turning it around. He always loves to make a situation that seems so bad, to be better and glorious. This is why you can see a prostitute turn to God and her life will affect more lives than the person who has always been a saint all her life. This is why you can be surprised at a man whom the world would have concluded will die poor suddenly change condition overnight and he is commanding companies.

God.s Condition for You To Prosper

Does the Lord plan that we will prosper? Yes! But how does He plan that we prosper? There is a condition to achieving the God-kind of prosperity. If you fulfill the condition, God will bless you. In Corporate Organizations, when people are given targets and they meet that target, they get rewarded.

Once I received an email from my company.s Head of Operations. In the email, the HOO asked me to send him list of people who had done well in the company; they were eligible for an all-expense paid trip to South Africa. Just like that. But with a condition attached to it: the eligible staff had to be people who had worked to deserve it.

How do you meet God.s condition to be

blessed? The Bible says they that seek the Lord shall not want anything good thing. If you do not want to lack any good thing, you must seek the Lord.

2 Chronicle 26:5 reads,
> **He sought God in the days of Zechariah, who had understanding in the visions of God; and as long as he sought the Lord, God made him prosper.**

As long as Uzziah sought the Lord, God prospered him. As long as he did not go back from seeking God, God kept making him to prosper. No wonder he became a king at age sixteen and he became one of the greatest kings.

2 Chronicles 26:15 reads:
> **And he made devices in Jerusalem, invented by skillful men, to be on the towers and the corners, to shoot arrows and large stones. So his fame spread far and wide, for he was**

marvelously helped till he became strong.

God so prospered Uzziah he even invented war machines. He sought God and God kept prospering him.

But his story did not end well. 2 Chronicles 26:16 reads:

> **But when he was strong his heart was lifted up, to his destruction, for he transgressed against the Lord his God by entering the temple of the Lord to burn incense on the altar of incense.**

As soon as a man starts to think he can leave God behind, no matter who he is, he is definitely going to fall. God will always exalt the humble and disgrace the proud. It doesn.t matter how long such proud person has been walking with him, God has no favorite but everyone who honours Him become His favorite.

As long as Uzziah sought God under the hand of Zechariah the Prophet, God made him to prosper. But the moment he felt he could do it himself, he was struck down with leprosy and shamefully hurled out of the temple.

What Does It Mean To Seek The Lord?

1. Delight yourself in the things of God, "Thus speaks the LORD of hosts, saying: .This people says, "The time has not come, the time that the Lord.s house should be built.". "Then the word of the LORD came by Haggai the prophet, saying, ["Is it] time for you yourselves to dwell in your paneled houses, and this temple [to lie] in ruins?" Now therefore, thus says the LORD of hosts: "Consider your ways! "You have sown much, and bring in little; You eat, but do not have

enough; You drink, but you are not filled with drink; You clothe yourselves, but no one is warm; And he who earns wages, Earns wages [to put] into a bag with holes." Thus says the LORD of hosts: "Consider your ways!
Haggai 1: 2-7

When your delight is in the things of God, you cannot escape God.s blessing. What are the things of God you should delight yourself in? You must delight yourself in Bible study, meditation upon God.s word, fervent prayers, listening to holy songs and fellowshipping with holy brethren. The more you talk to God about everything in prayer and the more God talks to you during meditation, the closer you get to Him; and remember that we said earlier that God.s presence with a man is what secures blessing for him.

If you are a wise Christian, you will always be looking for opportunities to be close to God, through engaging in all the spiritual disciplines mentioned above, and so doing,

God will always bless you. Actually, you walk in blessing to the extent that you appropriate these spiritual disciplines (Ps. 1:1-3); because what keeps you in the blessing are these disciplines that you engage in.

Jesus Christ said in John 12:26,

"If anyone serves Me, let him follow Me; and where I am, there My servant will be also. If anyone serves Me, him [My] Father will honor.

When your concern is how God.s concern will be fulfilled, God will make your concern His concern. The instant Solomon asked what was paramount in God.s heart wisdom to lead God.s people God blessed him with all that he didn.t ask for. I have found that God blesses people who seek His concerns far more than he blesses people who are only concerned about themselves. God may bless a selfish man, but it won.t be anything compared to what He will give the man who is concerned about God.s and other.s interest.

115

God.s first concern is that you will look like Jesus and His second concern is that your life should bring people to Jesus. When you look like Jesus in all things, more people can be encouraged to come into the Kingdom of God (Gal. 1:15-16; John 17:3; Phil. 3:10; 2 Cor. 5:15; 2 Cor. 5:18; Acts 20:24). If you are concerned about these two things primarily that you look like Jesus and you minister Jesus to others God will always keep you blessed.

It doesn.t matter where you find yourself, whether your workplace, family, or church, as long as God.s glory and interest is what you are always concerned about, and you serve Him diligently, God will never let you be left behind. If you serve Jesus, as the Scripture says, God will honour you. He certainly will!

2. Live By The Word of God
"This Book of the Law shall not depart from your mouth, but you shall meditate in it day and night, that you may observe to do

according to all that is written in it. For then you will make your way prosperous, and then you will have good success. Joshua 1:8

If your life is not controlled by the Word of God, you cannot secure a firm hold on God.s blessing. God.s blessing is powered by a constant obedience to Him, for it is in obeying God that God stays with us. The moment a man goes beyond what Christ taught and lived, God is no longer with him (2 John 1:9-11). A man who makes God.s word his first consideration and his final authority will always have God.s blessing follow him, as the day follows the night.

Joseph could not have secured God.s blessing for himself if he had not been obedient to God. King Saul brought ruin upon himself because he would not obey God completely. Samson could have become a very great man who lived long, but disobedience to God.s commandment cut short is life and destiny.

There is nothing more dangerous than a man living contrary to God.s word. We see this very strong example in the case of Adam and Eve in the Garden of Eden. They only disobeyed God once and that was it.

The Psalmist speaking in Psalm 119:161 wrote,

> **Rulers pursue me for no reason, yet I am more afraid of disobeying your instructions. N E T translation.**

And Isaiah 8:13 reads,

> **The LORD of hosts, Him you shall hallow; [Let] Him [be] your fear, And [let] Him [be] your dread.**

If you make up your mind that God.s word will be all you live by, your life will never be short of God.s blessing. No one, I repeat, no one who has ever followed God.s word and lived only by it has ever had any reason to regret it. There is not a single regret for you if God.s word is what you consider first in all matters and having found His word, you live by it.

Psalm 119:165 even confirms it,
**Great peace have those who
love Your law, And nothing
causes them to stumble.**

As long as God.s word is your absolute,
nothing will make you fall. I didn.t say that;
that.s what the Bible says, and the Bible is
absolutely correct about that. Do what the
Word of God says in everything and you
will see your life rolling over in blessing.

3. Love God

**Jesus replied, ".You must
love the Lord your God with
all your heart, all your soul,
and all your mind.** Matt
22:37

In a story told by Archdeacon Farrar, after
the siege of Rome in 1849, Garibaldi issued
this appeal to his followers: Soldiers, your
effort against overwhelming odds have been
unavailing; I have nothing to offer you but
hunger, thirst, hardship, and death; let all

who love their country follow me.

Hundreds of Italian youths followed him, because they loved him and because they loved their country; and, therefore, they could endure trial with greater joy than any selfish pleasures could bestow.

Devotion to God is a commandment; not a choice (Deut. 6:5; 10:12). It is a command; the greatest of all laws. Because devotion will always require love and attention, we are required to love God and be devoted to Him above all else.

Why is loving God above all else a commandment? First of all, you must understand that God is not a self-centered God (1 Cor. 13:5 1John 4:8, 16; Jer. 29:11). God will never do anything because He is first concerned about Himself. He does not put Himself first. He does all things because He is first of all concerned about you and He wants the best for you.

Therefore, if He tells you to love Him with all your heart, it is because He loves you deeply and wants the best for you. When you love God affectionately and your emotions, will, and reasoning (way of analyzing things) are controlled by your love for God, all other things will fall in place for you.

This is why it is important to love God. For example, if you truly love God, your decisions will always be controlled by what God says and how He views things. You will always be concerned about what is best for Him and even when other persons are misbehaving, you will be careful not to misbehave; because God is your first love and you don.t want to break His heart.

John 14:15 reads,
"If you love Me, keep My commandments."

The reason why most church workers misbehave is because they do not love God. They may profess to love Him but their actions prove otherwise. For example, you cannot love God and you will come late to church. This may appear too small, but love proves itself first in little things; and with God, if you are faithful in little things, He will consider you faithful in much.

Whatever directs your love (affection, heart) directs your will, emotions, and reasoning. When you love God with the whole of your heart, and you prove it by your actions, your life will be stable and you will enjoy His blessing. Every father reserves his best for the son he loves; God will always reserve His best for you if you love Him.

Loving God is the greatest road to manifesting. This is a life God wants you to live; a life of manifestation. He wants you to manifest, so that, like our LORD Jesus Christ, you may keep taking control over the devil and his works around you (1 John 3:8). Love God above all else and He will keep making you to manifest. You will manifest!

Chapter Five

AWAKE AND BEGIN TO MANIFEST

Now I say [that] the heir, as long as he is a child, does not differ at all from a slave, though he is master of all. Galatians 4:1

There is no news when you have power and you are not manifesting. The will of God is that you manifest. The will of God is that your light should so shine before men that they would see your good works and glorify your Father in heaven.

Your life should be an example of glorious

123

feats to copy. Your life should set the trail for others to follow. Your life, as a child of God, should define for unbelievers how to live and what to believe. Unbelievers should see you and marvel at the greatness of God. It is your God-given inheritance to shine in this manner.

The Bible says that you are the light of the world, a city set on a hill that cannot be hid (Matt. 5:14). You are the salt of the earth. That means wherever you are, there must be sweetness. But as long as you, the heir of all these blessings, remain a child, you are not different from a servant, says the Scripture. Though he is Lord of all, he is not different from a servant since he would not stand up to take hold of what rightfully belongs to him.

What does it mean to be an heir of God? It means you have access to everything God has. The only thing that will hold you back from accessing all these privileges is when you are still a child. Being a child here has nothing to do with your physical age, rather it deals with your understanding of the Scriptures; the revelation of the truths in the

Word of God to you. To the extent that you understand what you have in Christ Jesus through the revelation of the Word of God is to the extent that you will be victorious in any aspect of your life.

Oftentimes, when God releases graces into our lives, we do not take the steps needed to activate those graces; most times, due to the ignorance of such graces within us. At that point, we are usually looking for external solutions when the real solution is right within us.

Until you wake up and rise up, most of God.s graces upon your life will not manifest. Most prayers you pray often require you take steps of faith to activate the results. We pray, God answers, but then we start to look around again for physical evidences that He has answered when we have His word to assure us that He has answered us (John 14:13-14).

It is like a man who prays for money and he is given a cheque but he refuses to go to cash the cheque, will he get the money? No. He can sit there, fast and pray and still the money won.t manifest, because it is not yet transferred to him. He must take steps to get the money; in this case, he should simply go to the bank.

Imagine a man who struggles to win a game in the Olympics and when it is time to get the medal, he complains he is too tired to receive it; he wants someone else to go in his place.

Why should you refuse to take hold of the victory God has already acquired for you? The time of harvest that brings manifestation is the time to be alive. Elijah told Elisha, You have asked for a hard thing. Nevertheless, if you see me when I am taken up, it will be done for you. You are not supposed to sleep in the time of harvest. A son who sleeps in the time of harvest brings shame (Prov. 10:5).

How Do You Start To Manifest?

1. You must possess the presence of God.
An assurance of God.s presence is all we

need to face all challenges of life. David.s confidence when he came to Goliath was the name of the Lord. He boasted in God being with Him and being able to destroy the Philistine giant, and God, Who will always honour the man who honours Him, honored David with a resounding victory.

In Judges 6:12,

And the Angel of the Lord appeared to him, and said to him, The Lord is with you, you mighty man of valor!

Gideon was hiding because the Midianites were oppressing the Israelites. When the Israelites would want to reap their harvest, the Midianites would not let them. They subjugated and terrified them until even Gideon was threshing wheat in a winepress just to hide it from the Midianites. The Midianites would wait and allow the Israelites to work, then they would come during harvest to take what the Israelites had worked hard for.

It is impossible that you wouldn.t have enemies surrounding you. Enemies will always surround you. But the promise of God is that He will prepare a table before you in the presence of your enemies (Psalm 23:5).

Your business is not with the enemies. Your business is to have the presence of God. Moses insisted that God.s presence must go with them or they are just simply embarking on a suicide mission.

A man was threatened by witches that he would be killed. On hearing this, he hurriedly traveled to the UK. He had just gotten to his room in the overseas and was about to look at himself in the mirror when he saw the eyes of the same witches staring at him through the mirror. He ran out of the house and unfortunately got into train tracks and was smashed to death. It is not about running away from your enemies. It is about having the presence of God.

For we do not wrestle against flesh and blood, but against principalities, against powers, against the rulers of the darkness of this age,

against spiritual hosts of wickedness in the heavenly places. Ephesians 6:12

Location is not the problem of your enemies. The only thing that can stop them is the presence of God. When you carry the presence of God, let the enemy come one way, he will flee in many ways. The Scripture says when the enemy comes in like a flood, the Spirit of the Lord raises a standard against him (Isaiah 59:19).

God never said they would not come to fight you, but that they will come one way and flee in several ways. What makes them flee is the presence of God.

The presence of God turns a man.s weakness to strength. The angel said to Gideon, The Lord is with you, you mighty man of valor! (Judges 6:12). The angel called Gideon a mighty man of valor because when you have the presence of God, you cannot be a weakling.

You are as powerful as the presence that you carry and you are equally as weak as the absence of God you have. When a man does not have God.s presence with him, he becomes mincemeat for the devil; but when he carries the presence of God with him, all the hordes of hell cannot withstand him.

Once, a powerful man of God in Nigeria was on an evangelistic trip when he was waylaid by armed robbers. He simply told them to submit their guns and get in the car with him so they can go preach the gospel together. They submitted their guns and immediately became evangelists. This is what having the presence of God with you and understanding its efficacy can do to you.

The presence of God will arrest the enemy. If you don.t have strength, it will turn you into a powerful man (Isa. 40:29). The next time they come to you, what they used to do that would naturally affect you, will cease affecting you. They would wonder why their charms are no longer effective.

This is because you now carry the presence of God. The absence of God is what makes the enemy to defeat you. The presence of

God is what makes you constantly victorious over the enemy.

With God.s presence, you will begin to do what you cannot do before. Divinity has replaced your human ability. You will be able to reach the height you could not reach before.

2. You need to look to God

I will lift up my eyes to the hills; from whence comes my help? My help [comes] from the LORD, Who made heaven and earth. Psalms 121:1-2

The Psalmist lifted up his eyes to the hill but his help did not come from there; his help will only come from the LORD. Everyone who looks to God alone will always have tremendous victory.

There have been times when you needed something urgently and you got it in a way you never thought you would, simply because you looked to God. This happened because God takes delight in His children when they wait for Him and look to Him alone. He said in Jeremiah 17:5,

Thus says the LORD: "Cursed [is] the man who trusts in man and makes flesh his strength, Whose heart departs from the LORD.

God is always very angry with the man who looks somewhere else for his help. If God must help you to manifest, you must look up to Him alone. One of the ways to test if you are looking up to God alone is when you have a need, who does your heart go to first? If your heart does not go to God first, you have an idol beside God.

A truly victorious life is a life that trusts God absolutely. It does not mean you stop working. It just means that you only believe God to give you the solution although you are working by faith.

When David and his men returned from a battle in 1 Samuel 30:1, they found their wives and children had been kidnapped by the Amalekites. Immediately, David went straight to God to ask Him if he could pursue, overtake, and if he would recover all. God told him he should go; he would recover all.

In 2 Samuel 5:23-24, David was about going into another battle and you would think, Since he spoke to God before about pursuing the Amalekites, he should not talk to Him again. He should just assume what do. But no, David still asked the Lord what to do, and God told him exactly what to do, which was much different from what God told him earlier before he attacked the Amalekites.

You see, a man who listens to God for everything will never miss anything good. When God is all you look to for everything, you will never ever be disappointed. He will always reward those who wait for Him. This is why when those who wait for God finally manifest, it will be a season of great honour for them.

As you connect to the Lord by looking at

Him, your weakness and your inability is exchanged for His strength and ability. You would be able to attain everything you are supposed to attain, because you are no longer striving by your own strength, you are now striving by God.s strength. If you can look at God alone, you can manifest and stay permanently in the place of manifestation.

3. Use the Grace God has given you
"And to one he gave five talents, to another two, and to another one, to each according to his own ability; and immediately he went on a journey. Matt 25:15

God is a faithful Father and according to His Word, there are graces He has given to you. You must begin to identify them and start to harness them. The graces you do not use will go away, just in the same way the muscle you refuse to use atrophies. Grace unused is grace abused.

In the scripture above, God gives to every of

His children graces He expects them to use. He gives the grace according to each one.s ability so that no one will have any excuse for not using the grace God has given to Him. This is why, even in the body of Christ, there would always be things you can do easily and effectively which other believers in your group cannot do. Remember the words of the Holy Spirit through Paul the Apostle to Timothy in 1 Timothy 4:14:

> **Do not neglect the gift that is in you, which was given to you by prophecy with the laying on of the hands of the eldership.**

Why must Timothy fan the gift to flames? The reason is because if he does not fan it to flames, the gift will be there; dormant and useless. His life and ministry, both of which could have been aided powerfully by that gift, would be shallow.

Can you now understand why some Christians are not everything they are supposed to be in Christ Jesus? They expect

God to be the Magician who does everything for them. They expect God to pray the prayers they should pray. They expect God to study their Bibles for them so they can know Him. They expect that God will magically carry them over whatever they need to do without a single responsibility from them.

This is not appropriate. This is a disorder. God.s purpose for creating us in His image (to dominate and rule all things) will be defeated if all we do is sit back and expect all things to fall in place by a simple wiggle of the wand.

Every grace must be cultivated. Every opportunity must be seized. Every instruction and condition needed to activate God.s blessings and victory upon your life must be carried out. Every grace must be cultivated, I say again.

This is why the Bible expressly says in 2 Peter 3:18,

But GROW IN THE GRACE and knowledge of

our Lord and Savior Jesus
Christ. To Him [be] the
glory both now and forever.
Amen.

If you do not grow in grace and in the
knowledge of the Lord Jesus Christ, the
result will be Galatians 4:1. Like an heir who
should inherit all things but still remains a
child, you will be living like a servant when
all things are yours already (1 Cor. 3:21).

God does not want this for you. This is why
He expects you to cultivate the grace of God
upon your life.

To grow in grace is to engage in all the
spiritual disciplines that help you grow
bigger in your spirit man until you manifest
all round. Personal bible study, prayers,
meditation, listening to holy songs, and
fellowshipping with holy people are all
disciplines you should take advantage of
and develop. All these spiritual disciplines
are graces you must develop so that all of
God.s goodness can come out of you and
manifest.

There is also the place of developing your skills and talent and even yourself. Just because you are a Christian does not mean you should stop growing secularly. I am often surprised at how too many Christians never read anything past their academic books and their bible. They never even attend business seminars or visit new places. This is quite shocking.

If you would be able to speak boldly and intelligently among kings and not mean men, you must be developing yourself. God has en-graced you with opportunities that you are responsible to develop; God will not come down to do that for you.

You would think Joseph was a dunce when he came to speak with Pharaoh, but the advice he gave to Pharaoh proved that he was not a dunce; he understood what he was talking about based on personal development. If you don.t develop yourself, you may manifest luckily, but you will not be able to sustain the manifestation for long.

Your manifestation will last as long as you

are constantly developing God.s graces upon your life, both spiritual and secular graces.

4. The Knowledge of God will guarantee the presence of God

The knowledge of God will affirm God.s presence for you. The more you know God, the more you are confidently assured of His presence with you. This is the reason why knowledge of the Scripture is mandatory for every believer.

The devil can only be terrified by a man who knows God. I am not saying you should know about God but that you should know Him and be sure He knows you. This is what guarantees constant victory.

> **"Those who do wickedly against the covenant he shall corrupt with flattery; but THE PEOPLE WHO KNOW THEIR GOD SHALL BE STRONG, AND CARRY OUT [GREAT EXPLOITS.]** Daniel 11:32

Those who know God will be strong and will do exploits. When Paul was trying to make fire from woods after their ship crashed on an island, a snake came out of the woods and bit him. I noticed that Paul did not even fret or pray about the snake. The Bible says he just shook the snake into the fire and continued what he was doing. This experience was so shocking to his onlookers that they thought he must be a god (Acts 28:1-6). This is what a working knowledge of God can do.

The Bible says the thief comes not, but to steal and to kill and to destroy (John 10:10). I have discovered that what you permit as a Christian is what you experience. If you believe you are a failure as a Christian, then you are a failure. If you believe you can never fail as a Christian, you can never fail. What you believe will always become your reality. This is why the more light dawns on you through God.s word, the more confident and victorious you become as a Christian.

Have you ever wondered why some so called

Christians cannot sleep at night the moment they hear the sound of a cat or something funny just distances from their window? I believe it is because they do not know that the Bible says God shall give His angels a special order over you, to accompany, defend, and protect you in all your ways of obedience and service unto God (see Ps. 91:11 Amplified).

That, God himself explained further in Zechariah 2:5, I will be a wall of fire all around her, and I will be the glory in her midst.. If God is already a wall of fire around you and if in addition to that, He has given you His angels to specially guard you, then what.s the devil that will attempt to fight through those barricades? Know God for yourself!

> **What then shall we say to these things? If God is for us, who can be against us?**
> Roman 8:31

As long as God is for you, no devil can be against you. As long as you are on the Lord.s side, growing in the knowledge of Him and avoiding sin, you will never be a prey to the enemy. It is very easy to crush the cub of a lion when it is all alone, but when it is with her Lion father, you dare not come near it.

If the word of God is working in you and it is enough for you, who can be against you? The sword that we use to hack down the enemy and his activities is the sword of the Holy Spirit, which is the Word of God (Ephesians 6:17).

Acquire a voracious knowledge of God.s word. Keep growing in that knowledge, and soon, you will secure a permanent, lasting place in destiny.

5. You have all you need to manifest

A woman was deported from Canada suddenly. She was devastated because every embassy she went to rejected her. Her traveling papers were so useless no embassy even wanted to see her. She attended a church meeting and was prayed for. By the following Tuesday, the Canadian embassy called her, and so did several other embassies. God showed up for her after intensive prayer. Prayer is one of God.s greatest provisions for you to win until you become victorious.

There is no excuse for you not to arise from your present position to your next level of grace in God because God has provided all that you need. He says in 2 Pet. 1:3,

> **"As His divine power has given to us all things that [pertain] to life and godliness, through the knowledge of Him who called us by glory and virtue."**

What are the things that pertain to life? Victory, blessing, promotion, breakthrough, etc. God has given you all that you require for life. It is time to take the fight to the enemy.s gate. It is time for you to stop hiding behind the curtain and start to take charge of your destiny.

It is time to take charge of your finances through standing up to act on God.s word and working diligently at it. It is time to begin to appropriate God.s word to all the opportunities around you so that things can start to work for you. You wouldn.t be happy if you died and realized, as you stand before God, that He had given you everything but you didn.t use it, would you? So it is better to step into all that God has provided for you here on earth.

If God has called you blessed and He says you are blessed in Abraham.s blessing because you now belong to Jesus, then the next time you are doing your work, don.t work like a beggar. Stop it! Declare God.s word over your job or business and start to see God.s word manifest over your life.

If your family isn.t experiencing the victory it should be experiencing, get into God.s word, soak them into you, and let those words activate victory in every aspect of your family. All things that you will ever need in your life are hidden inside God.s Word. Get into God.s word, feed it into your spirit, and watch the devil run away like a dog with its tail between its legs.

You can change your life with a single

revelation from God.s word. You can manifest within the shortest possible time if you will but believe God and go for the word.

Your life is meant for something great.
Your destiny is waiting for you to happen.
The world is waiting for you to manifest.
They can barely wait anymore.
Will you manifest?

Chapter Six

OVERFLOWING WITH THANKSGIVING

Now thanks [be] to God
who always leads us in
triumph in Christ, and
through us diffuses the
fragrance of His knowledge
in every place. 2
Corinthians 2:14

What follows every moment of victory is a shout of triumph. When God gave the children of Israel victory over the Egyptians, all of whom perished in the Red Sea, they sang

146

songs of victory (Exod. 15:1-17). Immediately God gave Goliath.s head into David.s hands and the battle was over, with the Philistine defeated, the children of Israel sang for joy because they had been victorious.

Thanksgiving is a consequence of manifestation. What naturally follows manifestation is a shout of joy and gratitude. When you have triumphed and God has given you rest from your fight, you will naturally sing for joy.

But thanks be to God, the Father of our Lord Jesus Christ, Who causes us to rejoice even before the victory comes to us. How is this possible? This is possible because God has assured us victory before we ever go into battle.

You are fighting in a battle that you are already victorious. This is the victory that Christ achieved for us on the cross and this is why we constantly live a life of triumph come what may.

How do you feel, going into a battle where

you have been declared the winner before you started out? You know you are going into a battle but there almost isn.t any reason to fight because you are going into the battle as a victor.

Actually, you are going into that battlefield to plunder the enemy. You are going into the battlefield to only show off your victory, take what.s rightly yours, and even take what good things the enemy may have left behind.

Have you ever watched a movie and at another time, when someone is watching the same movie, he says, "This actress will be killed." You simply shake your head and laugh because you have watched the movie before now and you are sure the statement is not true.

In the same way, our introductory scripture assures us that God always cause us to triumph. This means that it doesn.t matter what the problem is, victory is always assured.

You can go through every challenge with a

smile on your face and laughter in your mouth, knowing fully well that this is only going to be another victory added to your archive.

Your life should be a life overflowing with thanksgiving, because the Scripture has assured us that God always causes you to triumph. It does not matter what comes your way, every day is another opportunity to shout for joy.

Do you know why thanksgiving is a prerequisite to manifestation? It is because you can.t really prove that you believe God when He says you are already victorious if you don.t give thanks. I know the situation has not been resolved.

I know your promotion has not yet been announced, but I am absolutely sure that God.s word is true when it says that God always cause us to triumph. God will always see to it that all things work in your favour.

This is why you must rejoice at all times. Philippians 4:4 reads,

"Rejoice in the Lord always. Again I will say, rejoice!"

Why must you rejoice at all times? You must rejoice at all times because God is with you. Maybe you should at least take a moment to think about Who this God is.

The Bible says in Genesis 1 verse 1, "In the beginning, God...." This tells us that God has been there since the beginning of the world; since the beginning of your life, God has been there.

The Bible describes this same God as the giver of all wisdom and knowledge and understanding (Prov. 2:6). He is great in might and He is greatly to be feared (Ps. 89:7). He is the One Who has everlasting strength and nothing scares Him (Isa. 26:4). This is the same God Who says you should rejoice at all times, even when things are not okay, because He has given you the victory. Halleluyah!

David looked at Goliath and said, "You come to me with sword and arrow. But I come to you in the name of the Lord of

Host Whose name and army you defile." Goliath scoffed at him and said, "You tiny thing, I will feed you to the birds of the air". But David had understood the scripture: "I can do all things through Christ Who gives me the strength" (Phil. 4:13). Of course, alone by himself, David knew he would be conquered flawlessly. But in alliance with God, he was unconquerable.

Every mountain becomes a molehill when you are with God and every molehill becomes a mountain when you are without God. They say that no one achieve this kind of feat or that sort of feat where you come from or at your place of work, but you can reply with confidence and say, "I can do all things through Christ Who gives me the strength." Christ in you is the hope that you will attain glory.

Someone said it is the "Christ" in Christmas that makes it Christmas. Christmas without Christ is just rice and chicken. But the Christ in the Christmas is what we celebrate. It is Christ in you that makes all the difference. It is Christ in you that changes situations and turn them around for your good. Nothing tremendously good could come your way if Christ was not in you. This is what shocks your enemies and cause them to marvel at the progress your life is making. It is simply inexplicable.

If Christ is involved, it must be unexplainable. It must be beyond words. As words cannot describe the glory and splendour of God, so words usually cannot describe the greatness, especially as constantly revealed, in the lives of His children.

God revels in His greatness and magnanimity. He glories in showing forth His awesomeness in the lives of His children, so darkness and the sons of darkness can stand in awe of His sovereignty. It is Christ in you that makes you unconquerable and every problem before you lie low or dies before you; making way to become testimonies. This is why shouts of joy and victory can be sung in your house; God.s right hand will always do mighty things for you, because God loves and cares for you.

The economy of the country may be upside down and downright crumbling, but when you are in God, you operate a different economy. There can be no scarcity in the Kingdom of God where you belong, then I wonder where the scarcity will come from that will threaten you.

God, Who rescued you from the hands of lions and bears and tigers that wanted to tear your destiny apart before now, will yet again rescue you from this uncircumcised Philistine posing itself as an immovable mountain before you.

As a result of all these sure victories, you should give thanks in everything. Giving thanks always is not an advice. It is not a suggestion. It is a commandment from the Lord, as you read in the scripture below.

"In everything give thanks; for this is the will of God in Christ Jesus for you." 1 Thess. 5:18

When Jesus taught His disciples to pray in Matthew 6:5-14, the fulcrum upon which the prayer guideline sat was thanksgiving to God; acknowledging God.s majesty before asking for what we need. Now, when the Scriptures say, "Thy will be done on earth as it is done in heaven", the question therefore is: what is the will of God?

In Revelation 4: 11, we read:
"You are worthy, O Lord, To receive glory and honor and power; For You created all things, And by Your will they exist and were created."

The Scripture above proves that God created us for His pleasure. As a result, when man is giving thanks to God, he is fulfilling purpose. But if your life is not giving thanks to God, you repay God evil for all His good to you. This is dangerous because the Bible says in Proverbs 17:13, Whoever rewards evil for good, evil will not depart from his house.

When Should You Give Thanks?
You would think you should give thanks only when things are going smoothly. When you need N100, 000 and you get N500, 000.

When you seek admission into a small university and you are granted admission into a prestigious one; and also given the course of your dream alongside. When you are concerned about how you will be able to pay the tuition fee and you are told you are on scholarship.

When you are in dire need of a job and you get an offer for three beautiful ones, and you are confused which to choose. When all these happen to you, these are not only the periods to give thanks.
You should give thanks when the tides are against you as well. Because the God Who was faithful in good times will equally be faithful in bad times. He will always make all things to work together for your good.

The Scripture we read says, "Give thanks always for this is the will of God." The statement "for this is the will of God" baffles me, because it establishes thanksgiving as a commandment and not an advice or a suggestion. It means that no circumstance - ugly or beautiful - is an excuse not to give thanks to God. In everything, give thanks.

Does this mean that God is not mindful that there will be times when things are not normal; there will be times when things won.t just go your way? Is God thus inconsiderate by demanding such from us? Absolutely no! As God.s children, God wants us to know that He controls the affairs of the world, though the devil claims to own the world (Luke 4: 7). God wants us to know that, as His children, nothing happens to us that He doesn.t know about (Heb 4:13).

Thanksgiving is the key to the impossible. It is the assurance that you have what you are looking for because you serve a living God. Someone said if you have big faith but you believe in a dead god, you have believed wrong; but if your faith is big and you believe in a living God, then you will always win. Your God is a living God and He has promised to help you. He will lead you into a life of constant manifestation. This is why you must give thanks.

Everything else may have a condition attached to it, but thanksgiving has no condition attached to it. If you are in any trouble, what James 5:13 tells us to do is pray, but if you.re cheerful, give thanks. Based on 1 Thess. 5:18, when you are giving thanks, you are doing the will of God.

Why do people not give thanks? Why do they refuse to appreciate God; seeing this is God.s will and God will never negotiate His will with anyone? You may be thinking, God understands what I.m going through and so He understands why I should not give thanks. I can keep looking gloomy and downcast and have every right to never give thanks. He sure understands this is painful for me.

Oh no, Beloved, you are wrong. God will not understand. God is a great God and He knows what He is saying when He says you must give thanks always. In Philippians 4:4, Scripture says, Rejoice ALWAYS in the Lord. Again I say to you, rejoice. This again shows that rejoicing always in the Lord is a command, not a suggestion.

It says to rejoice in the Lord. That means the reason why you are rejoicing and giving thanks isn.t because the challenge has suddenly been rolled away, but because you are confident in the fact that God, your Father, is for you, and He will fight for you and you shall hold your peace (Exod. 14:14).

This Philippians 4:4 proves Exodus 14:14 that every battle you face as a Christian is not yours; it is the Lord.s. So stand still and rest; rejoice and give thanks, because this is a commandment He gives to you out of love and assurance that He will fight each battle for you. You shall manifest because God has promised you will, and thanksgiving is a gateway that ushers you into manifestation the realm of the miraculous.

CONCLUSION

aving read this book, I hope the pages have given you an epiphany and you are ready to accomplish all that God wants you to accomplish in Christ Jesus. The pages of this book have proven without doubt that God wants you to manifest, and the essence of manifesting is to show forth God.s glory. As much as it breaks God.s heart that very few of His children are actually manifesting financially (and even spiritually), He is supremely glad when some of His children decide they would manifest.

Manifestation is a guaranteed way you can put the devil in his place and shut God.s enemies up. Once your life begins to blossom spiritually, financially, emotionally, etc, you become a channel through which others can praise God.

When, at your place of work, all that you touch seem to always become successful, your colleagues will marvel at the glory of God in your life.

But the journey towards manifestation may be decked with dangers and challenges; all of which God has promised us we will always overcome. The good news about the life we have in God is that we are promised victory before we have even started to fight at all. This is why it so easy to rejoice even in the midst of battle.

It will shock you to know that Jesus constantly rebuked His disciples for unbelief. This was because they constantly forgot He, the I Am, was with them. He performed many miracles before them, just to show to them that nothing is impossible with God. It may have taken a while, but they finally believed.

You don.t have to take too long to believe that Jesus is for you and as long as He is in your boat, the storms can blow all they want, the winds can be boisterous as much as they want to, but Jesus will rise to still them all. You are created in God.s image and are made to manifest. The whole of heaven will back you to manifest.

When you manifest, you prosper. When you manifest, you achieve the breakthrough you have always wanted. When you manifest, you get the promotion. When you manifest, you step into glory and stay there. When you manifest, you enjoy good health.

God has all these designed for you in Christ and He is waiting for you to step into it. Let all your shackles fall and let your agitations turn into joy today, because you are created to manifest; and you will surely manifest in Jesus name.

The grace of the Lord be with you always. Amen.

Kunle Akinbowale

Signposts to Manifestation

Printed in Great Britain
by Amazon